CONCILIUM

concilium 1993/6

MASS MEDIA

Edited by
John A. Coleman and
Miklós Tomka

SCM Press · London
Orbis Books · Maryknoll

Published by SCM Press Ltd, 26–30 Tottenham Road,
London N1 and by Orbis Books, Maryknoll, NY 10545

December 1993

ISBN: 0 334 03023 4 (UK)
ISBN: 0 88344 8742 (USA)

Typeset at The Spartan Press Ltd, Lymington, Hants
Printed by Mackays of Chatham, Kent

Concilium: Published February, April, June, August, October, December

Contents

Editorial: What the Church Needs to Know about the Mass Media

Our readers, advisors and the editors of *Concilium* have, for years, urged us to devote a special issue of the journal to the topic of *mass media*. The media are too important culturally and socially to ignore. They shape our perceptions of reality. The topic of mass media is very large. Our special optic on the theme tries to put together the church and the mass media. We ask ourselves two basic questions:

1. What does the church need to know about the media to negotiate its use and to fulfil its mission of discernment about modern culture?

2. What contributions can theology or the church make to our understanding and use of the media?

Not so long ago, in France, Alain Woodrow, the long-time religious editor of *Le Monde*, wrote a book entitled *Information, Manipulation*.[1] Woodrow's title suggests both the promise and menace of the media. They afford information, increasingly make of our world one global village and, frequently, play a liberative role, e.g. in making available pictures of repression in Prague in 1989 or in South Africa or East Timor or Beijing. On the other hand, some thoughtful critics complain that the media trivialize world issues. They inform but also de-contextualize the information they give. Today, we become concerned about hunger in Ethiopia or riots in North Ireland. Next week, we move on to the Kurds and a kind of detached curiosity and mere spectator's role takes over. The cool media can leave us very detached, even distracted. For the key slogan to the way the media tends to recount the news is caught in the broadcaster's transition phrase, 'And now – this'. The media can tend to turn information into discrete units of this and that.

Manipulation, in Woodrow's title, refers to the naiveté of thinking that there is any purely neutral 'information'. A serious hermeneutics of the media has to ask questions about who controls the media, whom it serves (the purpose of advertisers? of the government? of the First World?). It would probe the question of the values embedded in the techniques of newspaper print, radio, television. Thus, in the first part of this issue, we address the media as a cultural and social phenomenon and look at some of the most important value questions and religious issues the media raise. John Coleman situates the sociological study of the media with its twofold tendency to argue to a determinative causal role of the media and, in culture studies, to stress how viewers actually negotiate meanings of their own from the media. This second approach minimizes the power of the media to manipulate us. Coleman raises the question how the media shape our public discourse in arenas such as religion and politics. John Staudenmaier, a specialist in the history of technology, tries to show, in vivid terms, how the techniques of the media actually reshape our world of sensibilities and our prime metaphors for experience. Form is as important as content, Staudenmaier reminds us, when we study media.

Joan Hemels introduces us to the important debates about the democratization of the media. Are they controlled by elites? What access do popular movements gain to the media? How does the control of the media affect the way news about the church gets told and reported? W. E. Biernatzki turns our attention to the issue of the cultural imperialism of Europe and the United States in world media. He reviews the problems and possibilities in bringing about a more truly international control of the media and a more just world media order. Finally, Miklós Tomka takes us to debates in Eastern Europe where new laws are being introduced to shift control of the media from government and party political control to more open access.

In the second section of this issue, we turn, more narrowly, to the church and the media. We say 'more narrowly', since the church must also be interested in a more just media world and in how the media shape, culturally, our public discourse. Indeed, the issues raised in the first part of the issue may just be the ones to which the church should pay *most* attention. In the second section, we invited two theologians, Johannes Metz and Gregory Baum, to share theological reflections on the media. Then, Paul Soukup presents a masterful overview of what the churches have said in official documents about the media. Is it competent? Is it interesting? Is it likely to have much impact on the media?

We also want to know better how the church, around the world, has actually used the media in creative ways. In some countries and places, for example, the church sponsors whole networks and is concerned with more than just explicitly religious broadcasting. We would like to know what values determine the choice of programming when this is the case. Are they just – or mainly – market values? How, for example in such countries as

The Netherlands with its Catholic Broadcasting Company (*KRO*) or in Taiwan, does the religiously sponsored news and entertainment programming look different from, embody a different world view from, commercial or state controlled broadcasting? Ottmar Fuchs addresses the issue of church use of the media.

Finally, we ask several authors to present us with case-studies of reporting of religious news in the secular press. Michael Russo shows how the media manipulated and distorted three very different churchmen's position on abortion. Russo is less interested in the issue of abortion, as such, than in how the media interprets church positions for the public at large. Kenneth Woodward of *Newsweek* tells us how he goes about choosing what to write about religion in a secular news-magazine. His tale is one of the constraints of the form of the news-magazine, the constraint of editors and deadlines. Arnd Henze, who makes documentaries for German television, recounts his experience of reporting religion on television. His story is more optimistic than Woodward's, as Henze stresses the freedom he is given to present an in-depth vision without having to worry about the self-interest of church officials who are trying to protect institutional interests.

In the end, throughout this issue, we try to provide our readers with three important end-products: 1. a better understanding of how the media work technically, how they shape the way we see the world and react to it; 2. attention to a hermeneutics of the media, how we need to 'read' it as a text and learn to negotiate our own meanings by 'talking back to the media'; and 3. the moral and value issues involved in debates about the media. We are interested, in what follows, not just in the *content* of the media but in the media as a *context* in which we live.

John A. Coleman
Miklós Tomka

Note

1. Alain Woodrow, *Information, Manipulation*, Paris 1991.

I · The Media as Cultural and Social Phenomena

The Sociology of the Media

John A. Coleman

In his important theoretical book about sociology, *The Constitution of Society*, the British sociologist Anthony Giddens suggests that sociology, typically, falls into two contrasting tendencies to reductionism. The first and most dominant trend in sociology tends to over-emphasize structural realities to the detriment of human agency. Stressing structure as that which pre-dates and constrains human agents through its pre-existing norms, roles and institutions, this first view can be called a kind of structural determinism. It is as if structures are massively given, all-powerfully constraining and, through the mechanism of socialization, determine consciousness.[1]

The main problem with this over-emphasis on a legitimate viewpoint which stresses structures as sanctions and channelling mechanisms which shape and cause human behaviour is that this approach cannot adequately explain human change. For a withdrawal of consent to structures and cynicism about norms can topple even massive structures, as the 1989 revolutions in Eastern Europe show. Human agency is also real. We are not merely the pawns of pre-given structures.

The second theoretical tendency towards reductionism in sociology stresses just this aspect of human intervention and agency. Here, too, however, there can be a kind of reductionism which insists on the almost *complete* social construction of all social reality. At its worse, this second viewpoint might play down socialization, the givenness and con-straining character of norms and roles which pre-date us and shape us. Not all structures are equally vulnerable to change and revolution, even if all are socially constructed. Humans may be symbol-making animals who devise a web of meanings in interaction and socially construct their worlds. But some humans have more power than others, can manipulate or dominate, can control the use of symbols. Human agents, after all, do experience society as recalcitrant to their desires and projected meanings.

Giddens insists that we try to combine both of these two approaches to sociology in a symmetrical and complementary way. On the one hand, there are social structures which pre-date and shape our consciousness and behaviour. Social structures do channel behaviour, act as rewards and shape human agency to their contours. Structures definitely shape, even if they do not totally determine, consciousness. On the other hand, structures do not exist as such – in some abstract world. They are built up, maintained, resisted and undermined, reinterpreted, reimagined and restructured by people in their everyday lives and work.

Not surprisingly, the sociology of mass media shows the same dual tendency towards these two types of theoretical reductionism. The primary schools of thought in sociological studies of media stress either the structures of communication within a political economy of capitalism or – in what have been called cultural studies in the media – focus on the activity of human agents who 'read' the 'texts' of the media and accept them at face value, resist or negotiate their own meanings. In this second view, communication is always a two-way street. The cultural meaning of media or communication and their content can emerge only as a mutual product from those communicating. Only over time can we know what a 'text' of the mass media really says.

I. Political economy, a culture of consumerism and mass society

The first, more structural view of media has dominated most work on the media. It stresses how media shape our consciousness. This first approach is already strongly present in the famous studies of popular culture associated with the Frankfurt School of critical theory. It is found in more recent works such as Noam Chomsky's *Manufacturing Consent* and Neil Postman's *Amusing Ourselves to Death*.[2]

This structural approach tends to stress how mass media feed into and reinforce the political economy of capitalism. The media help to create a 'culture of consumerism'. They aggregate audiences which are then sold to advertisers in the magazines, newspapers or radio and television. Mass media reinforce mass society. In this approach, much attention is given to cultural imperialism, e.g. the dominance of American film and television industries. Equally, attention is paid to hegemony of the media by a few large conglomerates in each nation of the industrialized West. A very few news agencies in France, Britain and the United States put their stamp on what counts as 'news' almost all over the world.

This first approach attends to how the media shape and control public discourse, what is sayable or important in society. The massification of human agency (the interchangeability of humans) comes to dominate through the mass and amorphous, yet passive, audience for mass media. This leads to what Herbert Marcuse calls, in a pregnant term, one-dimensional man.

Neil Postman's *Amusing Ourselves to Death* can exemplify this first approach for us. Postman chooses as his master metaphor for television and the other mass media Aldous Huxley's *Brave New World*. He fears less George Orwell's *1984* in which an all-powerful surveillant state in the form of 'Big Brother' somewhat nakedly oppresses us. Instead, following Huxley, Postman sees the media as a kind of drug, what Huxley called *soma*, which leads to simplification and a soporific lulling of consciousness. Paraphrasing Marshall McLuhan's famous epithet, 'the medium is the message', Postman asks that we attend to the ways in which various media inform and shape the content of public discourse. In this view, our media are our metaphors and our metaphors create the content of our culture.

Without doubt, television has become the dominant mass media. For the structuralists in media studies, this form of public discourse regulates, even dictates, the content of public discourse in modern society. As Postman puts it, 'The content of politics, religion, education and everything else that comprises public business must change and be recast in terms that are most suitable for television.'[3]

The one who controls the stories a nation tells, especially those which pretend to be the 'real' stories, the eye-witness news, has power. Television is dominated by imagery. Only stories which have film footage connected with them get shown. Television has increasingly shaped our politics and the image we have of reality. For example, only good-looking and pleasant people are allowed to read our nightly news on television (no one who is old, fat, bald or ugly need apply!).

As television has become the hegemonic media, print media have declined in their influence and formats. Many newspapers and journals have disappeared. Postman notes, 'They delude themselves who believe that television and print coexist, for coexistence implies parity. There is no real parity here. Print is now a residual epistemology and it will remain so, aided to some extent by the computer and newspapers and magazines that are made to look like television screens.'[4]

Telegraphy and mass media

Mass media came into existence in the nineteenth century in print form through the invention of the telegraph (and the photograph). The telegraph spanned great distances and speeded up the time interval for the spreading of messages of communication. In his classic meditation in the wilderness, *Walden*, Henry David Thoreau spied the danger in this new form of communication. 'We are in great haste to construct a magnetic telegraph from Maine to Texas but Maine and Texas, it may be, have nothing important to communicate to one another. We are eager to tunnel under the Atlantic and bring the old world some weeks nearer to the new; but perchance the first news that will leak through . . . will be that England's Princess Adelaid has the whooping cough!'[5]

Thoreau feared that mass media would introduce large-scale irrelevance, impotence and incoherence into his world. News would come to us which was de-contextualized. We would learn about people and things which did not fit into our world of everyday life. Postman comments: 'Telegraphy gave a form of legitimacy to the idea of context-free information, that is, to the idea that the value of information need not be tied to any function it might serve in social and political decision-making and action but may attach merely to its novelty, interest and curiosity.'[6]

Already the telegraph introduced a form of public conversation which was new and startling: the language was the language of headlines – sensational, fragmented, impersonal. 'News took the form of slogans, to be noted with excitement, to be forgotten with despatch.'[7]

In Postman's pithy view, 'the problem is not that television presents us with entertaining subject matter but that all subject matter is presented as entertaining'.[8] Television looks to the fashioning of performances, the management of impressions, rather than the elaboration of ideas. News tends to be presented in forty-five second sound and sight bites. 'When a television show is in process, it is very nearly impossible to say "Let me think about that" or "I don't know" or "what do you mean when you say that?" or "from what sources does your information come?" This type of discourse not only slows down the tempo of the show but creates the impression of uncertainty or lack of finish . . . Thinking does not play well on television, a fact that television directors discovered a long time ago. There is not enough to see in it. It is, in a phrase, not a performing art.'[9]

Television news

The idea behind television news is to keep everything brief and not to strain the attention of anyone. The news broadcast aims to provide constant stimulation through variety, novelty, action and movement. We do not have to pay attention for long to any one concept or character or problem. Complexity must be avoided, nuances are dispensible. Visual stimulation becomes a substitute for thought and verbal precision is not rewarded. This form of discourse has passed over to politics and expectations about all discourse. People are less patient with long sermons. From the television politician, too, we expect short and simple messages rather than long and complex ones. We expect drama rather than exposition. We feel that being sold solutions is better than being confronted with intractable and complex problems.

There are many questionable assumptions about this view of the mass media as giving rise to mass society, undifferentiated public discourse and a one-dimensional man who is, basically, a passive member of the culture of consumerism in late capitalism. 1. Audiences are never as undifferentiated and mass as this theory assumes. The very idea of an 'audience' as some collectivity is a total abstraction. People from different social classes, regions, cultures consume the text of popular culture and interpret it in their own ways. 2. Consumers of the mass media are not merely dupes and purely passive. 3. Products of the mass media are not simply cultural commodities but 'texts' which, like any other text, require reading and are patient of multiple interpretations.

II. Bringing human agency back in: the cultural studies approach to the media

The cultural studies approach to the media – a term which derives from the Centre for Cultural Studies at the University of Birmingham in England which pioneered this approach to the study of media – disputes the assumptions of a structuralist, political economy view of media. Against a political economy approach to media which stresses how the media reinforce a culture of consumerism and capitalism, this second approach notes that audiences are quite diverse, coming from a huge variety of social groups and sub-cultures. It also stresses that audiences discriminate and make critical judgments.

After all, twelve out of thirteen pop records fail to make a profit. The vast majority of films are financial losses which do not recoup costs, despite high advertising budgets. Indeed, what makes or breaks a film is old-fashioned word-of-mouth communication and enthusiasm among friends and colleagues. Despite all the efforts of promoters and schedulers, many expensive television series fail to capture an audience. Far from being the most powerful of capitalist industries, the popular culture industries and the media may well represent capitalism at its most vulnerable.

Cultural studies of television programming, for example, show that audiences prefer television programmes which present them with a menu of meanings from which they can choose. Viewers view selectively and can resist the covert messages of television. Thus, for example, in Eastern Europe, during the period of the Communist regime, many viewers could 'read through' the government claims, propaganda and attempts to manipulate public opinion. Similarly, studies show how voters in Zimbabwe resisted massive television attempts, orchestrated by the last white government of what was then called Rhodesia, to subvert the election of Robert Magabwe. Western viewers show the same tendency to resist, when necessary, and negotiate the meanings they take from the media.

People selectively see what they want in television shows. One study of Dutch television, for example, found that socialists in the Netherlands liked the American soap *Dallas* because they claimed its very excessiveness was a kind of satirical critique of capitalism at its most savage. Other viewers liked *Dallas* precisely for its glorification of the fast-lane life, for modernity, for what they took to be an icon of brash Americanness.[10]

Popular culture, then, is not a monolithic text. Thus, a study of an Australian soap, *Country Practice*, which dealt with youth unemployment, found that viewers in a working-class school felt that it confirmed their social experience: there was a shortage of jobs in the country; school qualifications seemed irrelevant for getting a good job; unemployment was a fact of their class life. Boys in a middle-class school, however, felt that the plot no less confirmed their social experience: unemployment, they thought, came largely because of the fault of the unemployed. If they stayed in school and received good grades, these middle-class students read into their watching of the soap the message that they would inevitably get good jobs upon graduation.[11] People selectively take the messages they are predisposed to hear from the media.

The cultural studies approach, then, stresses how viewers resist television messages and read television as a multiple message medium which is patient of multiple meanings. Thus, one study showed how Arabic viewers actually rewrote in their minds (and what they thought they had seen on television) the script of *Dallas* by making one main character in that soap, Sue Ellen, return with her baby to her father (as would be customary in Arab society) rather than to her brother.[12] Another study among Australian aboriginals found that they rewrote in their reception of it the popular film, *Rambo*, so that Rambo fitted into a tribal or kinship rather than a nationalistic relationship with those he was rescuing.

The multiple reality of mass media

Church people who want to understand the mass media need to remember the multiple functions of the mass media and of communication in society. The media connect people and ideas; they invent new patterns of knowing and valuing in society; they inform; they regulate behaviour, values and agendas. Finally, the media entertain. The media provide a ritual function by connecting people to their environment and to other individuals. They reinforce group identity and provide a common background to people of diverse classes, regions and cultures within a given society. People share together a common viewing or through television some common perspective on a national event of great scope (e.g. a coronation, the death of a statesman, an election, a national championship soccer match). The media standardize language usage and pronunciation.

In the end, the media both mirror and shape society. They tend to support existing institutions in society and pass on the assumptions and consensus of society. When people accuse the media of a conspiracy to impose secular and liberal ideas, the media insiders always answer by saying that the media mirror society. While this is true, they nonetheless shape society as well. Thus, as Paul Soukup has noted: 'The media heighten people's senses of immediacy. The excessive present tense built into TV and radio news (live coverage, fast-breaking stories and so on) discourages truly in-depth reporting and absolutely outlaws patience and a sense of lived history. Time becomes something to be filled up lest a moment go by without its new content. This immediately also facilitates a rapid shift of attention.'[13]

Three questions to the church

For church people who want to know what the church should do about media in our society, I would suggest the following three questions:

1. Following Postman and others in the structuralist school, we can ask what the media do to our concept of public discourse in society. If it becomes harder to have a true conversation with nuance because of the media's tendency to think in headlines, perhaps we need other forums of communication as the principal locales for important discussions, e.g. elections. Importantly, not all forms of discourse can be converted from

one medium to another. This is the permanent lesson to be learned from
Marshall McLuhan!

2. While it is possible for individuals in an audience to resist and
negotiate the meanings of the media, without further cultural literacy
about how the form of the media shapes content, this resistance will remain
purely individual. What can the churches do to improve media literacy in
our societies, to help people reflect on the content of the information we
receive on television and the ways in which we can be truly more inter-
active with the media by 'talking back to the television'?

3. What about the use of media for explicitly religious purposes? For
what purposes are the media best suited for religion? Television may
actually transform religious programming into something else (e.g.
entertainment). Listen to the words of Neil Postman on this issue:

> There are several characteristics of television and its surround that
> converge to make authentic religious experience impossible. The first
> has to do with the fact that there is no way to consecrate the space in
> which a television show is experienced. It is an essential condition of any
> traditional religious service that the space in which it is conducted must
> be invested with some measure of sacrality. But for this transformation
> to be made, it is essential that certain rules of conduct be observed.
> There will be no eating or idle conversation, for example. One may be
> required to put on a skull cap or kneel down at appropriate moments. Or
> simply to contemplate in silence. Our conduct must be congruent with
> the otherworldliness of the space. But this condition is not usually met
> when we are watching a religious television programme. The activities
> in one's living room or bedroom or – God help us – one's kitchen are
> usually the same whether a religious programme is being presented or
> *Dallas*. People will eat, talk, go to the bathroom, do push-ups or any of
> the things they are accustomed to doing in the presence of an animated
> television screen. If an audience is not immersed in an aura of mystery
> and symbolic otherworldliness, then it is unlikely that it can call forth
> the state of mind required for a nontrivial religious experience.
>
> Moreover, the television screen itself has a strong bias toward a
> psychology of secularism. The screen is so saturated with our memories
> of profane events, so deeply associated with the commercial and
> entertainment worlds that it is difficult for it to be recreated as a frame
> for sacred events. Among other things, the viewer is at all times aware
> that a flick of the switch will produce a different and secular event on the
> screen . . . Not only that, but both prior to and immediately following

most religious programmes, there are commercials, promos for popular shows and a variety of other secular images and discourses, so that the main message of the screen itself is a continual promise of entertainment.[14]

Not surprisingly, then, the executive director of the National Religious Broadcasters Association in the United States summed up what he took to be the unwritten law of all television preachers: 'You can get your share of the audience only by offering people something they want'. The question to religious people, however, is whether what television might deliver about religion (especially if it is made easy and amusing) might actually be another kind of religion than authentic Christianity? Clearly, if the churches desire to negotiate their own use and presence in and through the media, they will need to understand better how the media operate in modern society.

Notes

1. Anthony Giddens, *The Constitution of Society*, Berkeley 1984.
2. Noam Chomsky, *Manufacturing Consent*, New York 1988; Neil Postman, *Amusing Ourselves to Death*, New York 1986.
3. Postman, *Amusing Ourselves* (n. 2), 8.
4. Ibid., 28.
5. Henry Thoreau, *Walden*, Boston 1957, 36.
6. Postman, *Amusing Ourselves* (n. 2), 65.
7. Ibid., 70.
8. Ibid., 87.
9. Ibid., 90.
10. Ien Ang, *Watching Dallas*, London 1985. For a more detailed view of the cultural studies approach to media cf. John Fiske, *Television Culture: Popular Pleasures and Politics*, London 1987.
11. John Tulloch, *Television Drama: Agency, Audience and Myth*, London 1990.
12. Elihu Katz and Tamar Liebes, 'Mutual Aid in the Decoding of Dallas', in Philip Drummond and Richard Paterson (eds.), *Television in Transition*, London 1985.
13. Paul Soukup, 'Communication and the Media', 1985, in T. H. Sanks and John A. Coleman (eds.), *Reading the Signs of the Times: Resources for Social and Cultural Analysis*, New York 1993, 154.
14. Postman, *Amusing Ourselves* (n. 2), 119–20.

The Media: Technique and Culture

John M. Staudenmaier

'That which shortens the time of communication, and facilitates the intercourse between distant places . . . tends to counteract local prejudices, by enlarging the sphere of acquaintance. It perpetuates existing friendships and creates new ones by which the bonds of union are strengthened, and the happiness of society promoted' (*Postmaster General on the first use of rail cars for US mail, 1834*).

'Let me write the song the army sings and I will have the army' (*Mediaeval maxim*).

Public discourse: how do we live outside the walls of our private domiciles; how live as citizens of the larger world? The Postmaster General of 1834 rhapsodized as rail cars began hauling mail at speeds approaching twenty-five miles an hour on iron roads that would suffer the rains without impassible mudslogs. The daunting size of the United States helped him understand very early what the next century and a half would teach; fast-travelling information breaks the world wide open. Electronic networks mediate a world so instantaneous and multivoiced that we citizens of the late twentieth century are still learning how to live as citizens of the whole planet.

If the Postmaster General saw the potential of speed, the anonymous mediaeval sage understood how great is the power of those who design highly crafted messages for large groups. The idea is not new; actors, preachers and public speakers have recognized it instinctively. What is new, however, is the technical capacity to move information, not at the speed of a lumbering train, but at the speed of light. Morse Code inaugurated the electronic information age just ten years after railroading the mails began. As the technology matured, it took the form of electronic information networks, a radically different sort of public place, 'the broadcast point of power'. The technical capacity to send a message to millions of people – instead of to the hundreds or occasional thousands who listened to an orator – creates a place with so much potential influence that power brokers of every sort fight for access. Not for nothing do television advertisements cost small fortunes and public relations teams labour at spin control.

Thus, the information age shows us a Janus face. On one side, global information networks liberate from local prejudice. On the other, they create passive audiences. In what follows, I will try, by sketching media history with a few broad brush strokes, to identify some of the challenges that stem from this provocative, paradoxical tension between liberation and conformity. I will argue, in particular, that electronic media have been designed in structures which reflect the larger Western tradition that has been their historical context of origin, a tradition which for several centuries has seen standardized systems as better than political debate as a way to work out solutions to human problems.[1]

One final note is in order. In so brief an article I will assume that I and the reader share the conviction that the global consciousness that emerges from electronic media blesses us profoundly. Here, I will concentrate for the most part on the challenges that the media present if we are to live that blessing well.

From speed of body to speed of light, the new world of public discourse

In the village world before electronic networks, news rarely travelled faster than a horse could trot. 'The news' described a minuscule universe, my village and a surrounding countryside perhaps thirty miles across. Information from beyond those boundaries arrived, not as 'the news', but as 'the olds' and its form differed accordingly. Newspapers published correspondences from distant places, leisurely essays complete with subtle asides to interpret the unfolding events. Still, in my own town, I received the news as an active interlocutor. I could supply a host of nuances that the printed account only suggested, and if I did not like the way my editor told the story I could walk over to his establishment, or meet him at church, and tell him what I thought.

Beginning about 1870, the wire services began to change all that. In 1876, for example, if I lived in Chicago I might read about the 'Molly Maguire' trials hundreds of miles away in the eastern Pennsylvania coal fields. I would learn that 'the Mollies' were Irish miners conspiring to destroy the lives and property of mine operators. I would have read, only one day after if happened, that twenty-four were convicted and ten hung. I would now know, however, that later historians see the trial as a frame-up, that the key witness was a Pinkerton detective employed by the owners. The wire service news crafters did not tell me that and I, reading my daily paper, lived too far off to know more than I was told. Thus a simple, essential reality, my geographical distance from the lived event, renders me passive, too ignorant to raise serious questions.

If standardized news systems make it hard for me to learn more than they tell me, their economic structure makes it almost impossible for me to construct and communicate an alternative version to the public. High media costs tend to lock individuals and poorly funded groups out of public discourse. A recent exception demonstrates the rule. During the Reagan-Bush administrations, while mainstream media adopted the administration interpretation of Central America (i.e., struggling democracies in Salvador and Guatemala v. dangerous dictatorship in Nicaragua), a grass-roots network communicated an alternative version so effectively that it significantly influenced national policy. One has only to recall however, the extraordinary efforts by individuals, *ad hoc* groups, and churches to see how unusual this example is. Whatever my ideology *vis à vis* the media in a given instance, ordinarily I experience myself as isolated and powerless. Even when I shout at a particularly odious advertisement or newscaster's remark on television, it wears me out to imagine that I might change things. Media fatigue creates an individualism rooted in passivity. Because 'I' cannot generate a public version of events, and 'you' can't either, the *communal* act where our several perspectives interpret the meaning of events ordinarily eludes our grasp. The recent popularity of talk-shows in the United States demonstrates hunger for a say, but the format does not seriously diminish the broadcast power of the professional who receives and interprets the calls.

Television and lessons of childhood

Television baby-sits and teaches children. Its influence, in this key social role, is endlessly debated, but it seems clear that children learn at least two lessons which psychologically foster audience passivity. First, children need to acquire a habit of passivity to help them watch television without intolerable confusion. At some point they learn that talking back to the TV is fruitless; that those who seem to be conversing *with* them in fact only talk *at* them; that no one in TV's universe wants to be interrupted. To cope with this unsettling reality, children learn ambivalence about their capacity for intimacy, the inner ability to create talk that matters.

Television also protects its speakers from too much spontaneity. Typically, when a newscaster is caught in a rare moment of unrehearsed grief or anger, we are touched by the simple fact that the veneer of professional competence has been broken and a hint of human passion shows through. Before long, however, the system recovers and we once again witness men and women who, as they read the news, live out melodramas in soap operas, or celebrate the wonders of toilet paper, play their assigned roles with practised ease. Thus the second lesson: highly-crafted talk is better than spontaneous talk.

Television's highly-crafted, non-spontaneous style exerts pressure on us to compete with it. What does it mean to live in a society whose public voices sound so unlike our own? It is not as if human beings never before longed to present a refined image of themselves! The long history of theatre, oratory, cosmetics and fashion proclaims our desire to dress up for special occasions. Still, we know that our truest story runs much deeper and more mysteriously than our occasional highly-crafted moments can suggest. We live a rhythm of mystery and clarity, of ambivalence and coherence; we are eloquent and bumbling by turns. We know that we, and our public institutions as well, will not endure without affection for the unexpected and ambiguous, but the courage and sense of humour needed to tell our stories often wither in the presence of the media's implacably well-crafted voice.

The cultural evolution of standardization

Another way to understand these patterns of passivity is to see media networks and their audience as working elements of a standardized technological system. Standardization's governing idea, to solve problems by designing systems with precise operating constraints and then enforcing conformity to those constraints, has long historical roots in the West. It appeals to that side of us that takes offence at the messy and turbulent ambiguities of life. Mechanistically inclined philosophies as far back as the Greeks have offered conceptual models to guide the design of large-scale, bureaucratic governments. In the same tradition, aesthetic objects from automata that imitate animal life to horologues replicating the movements of stars and planets, the dream of clean, focused clearings in the tangle of unpredictable life has flourished.

For several thousand years, however, Western love of clarity and fear of chaos operated in the context of a balancing recognition that too much clarity is dangerous and that the uncertain dark is sometimes the necessary seed-bed of life and of vision itself. Job and Oedipus painfully learn that some questions cannot or should not be answered. The book of Job ends without an answer, its questions about the meaning of suffering finally silenced. Oedipus finds his answer, but, seeing what his history reveals, puts out his eyes. Likewise, the Western tradition of the holy dark, the frightening places in which visions are born and human purpose renewed, stretches from Abraham's vocational dream-visions and Jacob's night-time wrestling with the unnamed stranger to the Cloud of Unknowing and the Dark Nights of the mediaeval mystics, and Shakespeare's tender 'sleep that knits the ravell'd sleave of care'.

The intuition that uncertainty must balance clarity and the ambiguous temper the purposeful suffered periodic collapse when various communities broke out in vicious fanaticisms, such as Ferdinand and Isabella's ethnic cleansing of Jews and Muslims from Spain and the more violent excesses of the Inquisition. In such instances, love of clear boundary definitions drifted towards a savage lust for order.

Even during the worst of such excesses, however, the systematizing urge was held in check by a technological style which held precision measurement in only modest regard. However much one might long for the bright light of clean boundaries, the diurnal rhythm of day and night governed life. In a world of inadequate artificial light, night put an end to working time. Night prayers mixed fear of the dark ('Preserve us from violence and crises; keep our imaginations and passions in check') with affection for dimly-lit times of story-telling and rest ('Into your hands, O Lord, we commend our spirits'). Even during the daylight, the urge towards accuracy was limited by imprecise machines and instruments. To take one example from many, public clocks long showed only one hand, telling the hour but not the minute. In the course of the eighteenth century, however, improved clock escapements and temperature compensation enabled clockmakers to improve best accuracy from an already remarkable ten seconds per day to 1800's one-fifth of a second.

Two revolutions, the British industrial and the French political, created an unusually powerful hiatus in European culture near the end of the eighteenth century. During the two decades spanning the turn of the nineteenth century the French revolutionary republic dismantled civic and religious structures, only to be itself replaced by Napoleon's Empire. Meanwhile, French industrialists had begun inviting British factory masters and skilled artisans to cross the Channel and install the new

industrial system. It proved a powerful mix; the traditions of the Ancien
Régime died a violent death during the years of the Revolution, and later
attempts at restoration, particularly in church matters, were carried out
under the powerful influence of industrial capitalism. Where factory
masters tried to enforce precisely defined work rules, the church gradually
turned to similarly detailed codes of law and doctrine. Boisterous politics,
whether on the shop floor or in the Vatican, became increasingly suspect.

   The historian Patricia Byrne has identified a striking instance of the
pattern among the Sisters of St Joseph in France. Eighteenth-century
France was host to many tiny congregations of Sisters of St Joseph,
typically five to twelve members. Communities in larger towns and cities
differed dramatically from those in rural areas. Town houses conducted
their financial affairs, chose their places and types of work, and governed
their community lives with remarkable autonomy. The mostly illiterate
women in the country houses, on the other hand, ordinarily operated
under the tutelage of a town house sister with little autonomy. Both sorts of
community were called by exactly the same name, 'Congregations of the
Sisters of St Joseph', and both were considered independent organizations. Examples of similar nominal ambiguity could be multiplied. To
call these tiny groups by the same name required a tolerance for conceptual
and behavioural ambiguity that did not survive the Revolution intact.
However, as the Sisters of St Joseph were restored after their decimation
during the Revolution, the pattern of amorphous co-operation between
independent communities gave way to centralized government. Thus, by
1840, the Congregation of Lyons ran over two hundred separate houses
from its central seat of governance. Communal life began to be regulated
by detailed codes very like the factory work rules then revolutionizing
manufacturing. Gradually, while instrument makers revolutionized the
world of precision measurement and quantitative analysis, religious and
cultural leaders began to read the holy dark out of the Western canon.
Mysticism went the way of playful ambiguity and sensuality, all subject to
the scrutinizing eye of the new guardians of uniformity.

   Standardization as an ideal emerged from this same revolutionary
world. Perhaps its most striking early manifestation, French weapons
manufacture, reached the United States via friendships among French and
US officers and appeared in the 1816 law requiring the US Ordnance
Department to pursue the goal of producing small arms 'according to the
principle of uniformity'. Not surprisingly, the introduction of standardization in manufacturing became a battle-ground between a world of
shop-floor politics where skilled workers contested with owners for what

each considered legitimate rights and a new order where experts designed systems so complex that the unpredictabilities of debate and compromise could be replaced by conformity. When, therefore, the first national wire service began to revolutionize public discourse in the 1870s, its inherent need for audiences schooled in the virtues of conformity to well-organized systems reflected a much larger societal change, the maturation of industrial capitalism in the West.

Electronic media: challenges and blessings

The Janus face of media, therefore, liberation from localized myopia and conformist passivity together, is the face of the culture we carry within us. Critical thinking about media tendencies, as in the preceding pages, gets us nowhere if it leads toward a romantic fantasy of village life that disconnects us from public responsibility in the world we have inherited. How, then, might we engage these powerful technological and cultural forces creatively? We might begin by treating them as signs of our times and, following the injunction of Jesus, work at learning to read them. When we see technologies as cultural options rather than inevitabilities, they help us understand how grace and temptation work in our particular culture. Space prohibits an extended discussion, but a few observations about media challenges to faith can serve as a conclusion.

Electronic geography: the media challenge us to live in an interconnected world where once-local events, such as tribal warfare in Somalia, have global consequences. We can no longer say that remote tragedies happen without our knowledge or beyond our reach. Indeed, we are implicated in these events through the tangled web of worldwide economic and technical interconnections. How, then, pay attention to world events without going numb from overload? It is a deceptively simple but crucial question. The electronic media only operate as an imprisoning closed circle – conformist audiences locked in step with autocratic message-makers – in so far as the social dynamics I have sketched above induce fatigue and self-contempt. Transformation from passive audience to active citizenry requires courage and willingness to contemplate the world patiently; then it can teach us how to engage in its affairs.

Electronic time: When a world organization, an international corporation or even the Roman Catholic Church, changes from speed-of-body to speed-of-light communication, how ought models of governance to change? Two hundred years ago an authoritarian message from headquarters to another continent took so long in transit that recipients had great latitude in how they received it. Slow travel meant time to ruminate and consider one's response. In today's tightly coupled world of instantaneous communication, authoritarian rhetoric has drastically different implications for governance. How might we legitimate rumination time for electronic messages? How, in the language of the previous observation, might we find the courage needed to contemplate the implications of the messages we receive long enough to learn a response that will matter?

These two issues can operate either as graces or temptations. Both the speed and spatial range of messages tempt us, as should now be abundantly evident, to passivity and disengagement from the decision-making processes at work in the world. At the same time, they can challenge us to learn a spiritual discipline that would liberate us from passivity. Such a discipline is at once public and contemplative; it depends on courage in the face of intimidation and renewal of inner resources in the face of fatigue.

One way to start would be to honour story-telling and listening to stories. Electronic media tend to erode the art of storytelling partly because media discourse conveys 'new' information at such a pace that our stories feel out of date before we find time to tell them, and partly because highly polished media talk intimidates amateur story-tellers. Nevertheless, no culture can long survive when its members lose their appetite for one another's stories. Perhaps the ancient discipline of fasting could be applied to electric and electronic technologies. How might we be changed if, once a week, we disconnected our telephones, radios, televisions, electric lights and computers? Such fasting might help create a place and time for contemplation and for the intimate play of storytelling.

Such a practice, so manifestly modest and domestic, reveals the central paradox of a world woven together by centralized, speed-of-light information systems. Public citizenry requires personal intimacy. Individual people will not retrieve their capacity for public citizenship unless they find ways to renew their inner selves on a regular basis. Citizens run the risks of the public order – the debate and the alert study of events that debate requires – only when they recognize their inner authority as human beings, and that takes patience, a sense of humour, courage and hope. If, then, our electronic technologies compel us to live on an instantaneous planet, we must learn to live in this new order gracefully. Honouring storytelling would be a good place to begin.

Note

1. I will describe cultural and technical patterns that originated in Europe but flourished in the United States, my primary area of research. Readers from other socieites will do well to adapt these observations to their own circumstances. Of course, given the economic power of US-dominated media networks, such a case study may prove worthwhile in its own right.

Democratization and Control of the Media: The Issues and the Debate

Joan Hemels

Introduction

In the week of 11 January 1993, Dutch mass media of different social perspectives and various persuasions covered the quinquennial visit of the Dutch bishops to the Vatican. At this so-called *'ad limina* visit' the situation of the church province of the Netherlands was examined in a report which was descriptive, analytical and evaluative.[1] Among other things the report highlighted the problem that the Netherlands no longer has 'Catholic media'. This cannot be seen as a fortuitous or isolated remark. The underlying thought here is clearly that bishops in a highly secularized society should have ready access to media which are to be regarded as 'Catholic'. And these media ought also to be able to serve to communicate the faith, something which in the Netherlands and elsewhere has become so problematical.

Attention to the mass media as cultural and social phenomena with an influence on the life of people who can no longer be addressed by traditional institutions is not unique to the bishops whose sphere of work lies in the Netherlands. In other contexts, for example in politics, there is also a temptation to make the media (once again) responsible for anchoring threatened social norms in the hearts of the population, especially the young. Moreover complaints about a blurring of social norms often point the finger at these same media, except that in this case an all too schematic distinction is made between the 'good' and the 'bad' organs of the press, broadcasting, or whatever.

The visit of the Dutch college of bishops to the Vatican in January 1993 is sufficient occasion for a case study with special reference to the media content of this event. Here I shall use the meeting in Rome simply as an instance of the problematical way in which the media in fact function in a democratized political and socio-cultural context. The line of the argument is that even under these relatively favourable conditions it is extremely difficult to bring about changes in an ideal direction. The church also experiences this and is more opposed than many other institutions to the uncontrolled and uncontrollable media explosion which is taking place worldwide. This is evident from the recent church statement that a different 'media performance' is desirable from the media system. The church's opposition is to be praised, but it is highly questionable whether its wish will ever be granted.

Interference in the media through regulations imposed by the authorities seldom leads to the desired result at the level of content. Moreover, the spirit of the age is opposed to interference in the content of the media by the authorities, by a church, a political party, a trade union or a commercial pressure-group. There is less and less talk of effective control in some form: an authority which understands the spirit of the time will simply impose a basic framework within which the media are to function. At the same time, the margins for democratization in the sense of easier access of all kinds of minorities to the really important media at a time of increasing commercialization seem to be extremely narrow.

Finally, democratization of the media is also understood as granting journalists and programme-makers in their service some say and some role. This is a concern which marks dealings between all kinds of managements and their staffs in modern Western society. The media pay attention to it, but little evidence of the concern can often be seen in the structure and organization of these media. If journalists and programme-makers have achieved some shared participation in particular media, this does not automatically mean that their public also has a share in them.

Shaking off the burden of the past

The deliberate remark about the loss of Catholic media in the report of the Dutch bishops can also be interpreted in the light of the past as being somewhat malicious. If that is the case, this remark gives the impression of being a nostalgic longing for a past time when bishops could exert influence formally and informally on Catholic journalists and editors. To control the content of, for example, Catholic newspapers, with the support of the church's law about books they appointed censors.

Since the 1960s in the Netherlands supervision of the media and media managers by the church has become unthinkable. With the end of the sharp divide between church and state, above all the Catholic press went its own way. This was in the direction of a de-ideologizing, certainly of traditional Catholicism with its respect for authority. The main result was a far-reaching market orientation accompanied by commercialization, which in some cases ended in the abyss of liquidation. This process took place in a period of twenty to thirty years, in other words of a generation of journalists, editors and readers.

Nevertheless, the reception of the Dutch bishops by the pope cannot have escaped any television viewer or newspaper reader in the Netherlands. The reporting of journalists from press bureaus, radio and television companies and print media led to extensive coverage, even in media which could not be described as Catholic. Dutch people, regardless of their church affiliation, could make their own free choice in forming their opinion from interviews with bishops, background information to the report, and commentaries on how the visit affected the position of the church in the Netherlands. Without having their own (Catholic) media which they were able to control, bishops, like other citizens in positions of responsibility, as it were lined up before journalists to join in the public debate. To their delight or disgust journalists sometimes also lined up before bishops because they wanted something from them which could be news or which for some reason or other was worth reporting. Journalists now no longer know the meaning of fear of authority, so their behaviour can sometimes seem shocking. One has to learn how to deal with the representatives of today's media. That certainly cannot be denied.

Freedom of expression in the Netherlands means that there is no preventative control (censorship). Every citizen has the right to give an opinion freely, whether he or she is a journalist, a politician or an ordinary citizen. A text or other form of expression can be condemned as unlawful only after it has been published. Everything is possible, but not everything is permissible. For example, slander and racist statements are criminal offences. These restrictions are accepted without discussion by the vast majority of Dutch people. Anyone in the Netherlands who wants to complain about the content of print media or broadcasts is free to go to an independent arbiter. It is no use going to a minister or a bishop. As is evident from recent cases, ministers will even dissociate themselves from statements by members of parliament.

A bishop, like any other citizen, can state publicly what he does not like about the media in general and particular press organs or broadcasts in particular. However, there are only a few recent examples of such critical comments by Dutch bishops, one of them being from Bishop Bär. This media bishop in particular makes it increasingly evident that the journalists cannot always or easily be accused of failures in communication. In an interview with the Christian daily *Trouw* of 14 January 1993, given on the occasion of the *ad limina* visit, Bishop Bär remarked that people were often ill-prepared for the great flow of information about views on life. He immediately added: 'I don't blame the media for this, but people are ill-prepared. They don't really pay attention, and get upset.'

The church's access to the media

Many people were surprised that the *ad limina* visit as such was made a media event. A visit of the Dutch college of bishops to the pope is different from, and of less interest than, a visit of the pope to the Netherlands. On returning to the Netherlands the bishops may have been surprised at the stir that their visit to Rome had caused in the media. All in all they clearly still had access to the media, regardless of whether this bore the title 'Catholic' or not. This is less a matter of course than it seems, certainly when one thinks of countries where there can be said to be open anti-clericalism or rejection of the church and faith.

In the Netherlands, too, coverage of such matters is by no means automatic. Over the last twenty-five years there, barriers between church and state have been increasingly blurred, with deconfessionalizing and de-ideologizing as concomitant phenomena. Secularization as a process by which sectors of society and culture have come to be less and less dominated by religious institutions and symbols is even older. For many Dutch Catholics the authoritative statements of the church *magisterium* slowly but surely lost their power after the Second World War. Decisions made on conscientious grounds became crucial. Sociologists of religion and historians have recently mapped a global cultural shift and a change of mentality in Dutch Catholicism, but cannot give a satisfactory explanation for it.

The development sketched out above has had far-reaching consequences for the way in which the media in the Netherlands treat topics relating to the church, church life, faith and religion. For this very reason the Dutch bishops now see the disappearance of all daily papers and most journals with a marked Catholic character as a problem. Regardless of the fact that they are rather late with their complaint, the question arises whether they are quite right. We can see how in certain circumstances the statements, actions and appearances of Dutch bishops can lead to media coverage. Neither the church nor its leadership has been silenced by journalists. However, they can no longer be said to have a privileged position in most media. In the struggle for the attention of the media, church leaders must vie with captains of industry, politicians, stars of show business and criminals. And independent journalism does not need to include among its tasks the encouragement of, say, the communication of the faith.

A closer look at the role of the mass media

In their report to the pope and the Vatican authorities the Dutch bishops write that the mass media determine what the news about the church is and how that happens. Any political leader or director of a multinational corporation can claim this from his own experience. Amazement or irritation about it is in place. In communications science this independent fulfilment of their task by the media is studied in the framework of the agenda-setting hypothesis and the gatekeeper function of media. According to the first concept the media play a role in bringing about 'differential attention to issues and objects in the world'.[2]

The second concept is above all concerned with the relationship between the media and their sources. In this connection Denis McQuail considers 'the question of imbalance between suppliers and media takers of information or other content. Some sources are more powerful than others or have more bargaining power because of their status, market dominance or intrinsic market value. This situation is reflected, for instance, in the privileged access of the more politically and economically powerful and the favoured position of richer media and media systems in the world. Media organizations are far from equal in their degree of access to sources which can further enhance their position.'[3]

Those who control or dominate the media can make their influence on content felt most. However, outsiders are not wholly abandoned to caprice or arbitrariness. They can also deliberately and systematically bargain for the attention of journalists and programme makers. Public relations from businesses is one way of exercising influence from outside on the content of media messages and even generating them. Authorities can make use briefings of media representatives for the same purpose. There is a permanent stream of information from business and public government. The political parties, all kinds of social organizations with specific interests, and action groups know the way to press bureaus, print media and radio and television programmes. In this connection the term 'news management' has come into being: anyone can try to get into the news, if this can help his or her reputation or lead to free publicity. Anyone who is afraid of damage has to take just as much care to avoid the attention of the media.

In addition to public relations the purchase of media space (advertising) and sponsorship (on radio and television) are more or less usual ways of getting to the public of selected media. This can happen with a view to selling goods and services, but also for realizing an aim of communication, like increasing knowledge of a brand name or improving an image.

The Dutch bishops give the impression that they are not wholly ignorant of the content of the chapter 'Media Institution, Organization and Role' in handbooks of communications science. At any rate, in their report they note that the way in which the media culture is produced can be counter-productive for church and faith. By contrast, they think, a good use of the media would be to help to increase the 'social plausibility' of the church's message. In the bishops' view, people can take this message more seriously if it has 'less totalitarian pretensions'. In other words, in forming their opinions and defining their attitudes, individuals of our time who have come of age depend on media messages which leave room for discussion, different interpretations, views and feelings. Forcing opinions does not work.

Towards a 'culture of dialogue'

The Dutch bishops recognize in their report to Rome that their communication with a number of groups falls short. In this connection they also make explicit mention of journalists, not referring specifically to Catholic journalists. They also inform the pope and Curia that a strengthening of 'the formal structures' of authority is not enough to improve communication with the groups indicated. At all events on paper they dissociate themselves from a strongly hierarchical communication structure, 'from the top to the bottom', with the character of a monologue. This explains their option for 'the culture of dialogue' as 'a primary missionary attitude in present-day Europe'. Here the Dutch bishops follow the direction of the pastoral instruction *Aetatis novae* which appeared in 1992.

In a commentary in the Dutch Christian, originally Protestant, newspaper *Trouw*, a critical mark is put against the episcopal statement of intent. Not every Dutch bishop is said to have approved of such a 'culture of dialogue'. Moreover the bishops are said not to have been able to give prominence to the condition formulated in the report that their conversation partners support them in their specific responsibility within the church structure. If communication is to be successful in the interpersonal sphere or through the mass media, then the credibility of the parties involved in this process is an important condition.

Whereas the world is changing through democratization, the church still has little of an eye for this process. That is what makes an authentic dialogue so difficult. Moreover it has the tendency to assign tasks unasked to media which are not controlled and dominated by it. In this connection one might mention the requirement for dialogue in the world, the promotion of social progress and collaboration in evangelization (or re-evangelization). The 'service' of the media to individuals and cultures is a key term in the pastoral instruction *Aetatis novae* mentioned above. Michael Schmolke, one of the greatest experts on church statements about questions in the sphere of communication, including mass communication, wrote in reaction to *Aetatis novae*: 'The emphasis on service unavoidably raises the suspicion that here we have a return to the instrumental thought about the media characteristic of the period before Vatican II: the media as an extension of the pulpit, as a megaphone for the bishop.' Schmolke, who is Professor of Communications at the University of Salzburg, points out that while the church can use its own media as instruments of evangelization and the like, it cannot impose any tasks on the secular media. In his view these independent media should simply pick out of the life of the church what has news value in the public market. According to Schmolke, that comprises on the one hand demonstrably good actions, and on the other the conflicts which bedevil church life and in part arise from the fact that the church does not always act in the spirit of the 1971 *Communio et progressio*.[4] The idea was to bring this document up to date after twenty years with *Aetatis novae*, but this aim has not been wholly achieved.[5]

Consequently people continue to look for a change in the closed, strongly hierarchical culture of communication in the church which has grown up over the centuries. In a retrospective survey of twenty years since *Communio et progressio*, Johann Baptist Metz has discussed the church culture of communication since Vatican II. He makes clear that the socially divided and culturally polycentric world church runs the risk of identifying itself with a Eurocentric media culture. According to Metz, the church which needs (needed) so much time to see the significance of the processes of culture in its own sphere and outside it risks falling into a new trap. It could lose itself in the communication culture, which is rooted in a 'rational and commercial culture of power', and not have enough respect for the freedom and worth of others. In his view, identification with this Eurocentric structure and communication culture could further undermine the credibility of the church.[6]

The loss of Catholic media

The media situation which the Dutch bishops criticized in Rome needs some clarification. When writing about 'the media' the episcopal reporters were clearly thinking exclusively of newspapers. This was to undervalue other print media. Thus the *Katholiek Nieuwsblad* has appeared twice a week since 4 October 1983. The circulation of this markedly conservative paper continues to remain below 20,000. Other Catholic papers appear, including one Catholic weekly. This 'weekly magazine for church and society', *De Bazuin*, is a progressive counterpart of the *Katholiek Nieuwsblad* and has a circulation of about 5,000.

Moreover the Catholic Broadcasting Company (KRO), which was set up in 1925 as a foundation formally independent of the bishops, still continues to exist. With 610,000 members at 1 January 1993, the KRO has survived the changes in Catholic organizations and institutions which took place during the 1960s. The authorities give the churches in the Netherlands air time for radio and television programmes. The Roman Catholic church entrusts the filling of this air time to the KRO. There are periodical discussions with representatives of the college of bishops of the way in which the KRO fulfils this task. As an extreme sanction, in the case of a serious conflict with the KRO the bishops could withdraw their approval. However, this extreme course has never been resorted to, for all the tensions which there have been in the church province of the Netherlands in recent decades. Both parties have always successfully arrived at an agreement. Certainly the bishops follow with more than usual attention the way in which eucharistic celebrations are covered by television and radio. A text of the canon not approved by the Vatican can in itself cause problems.

The standpoint of the Dutch bishops over the lack of desired or desirable Catholic media in the Netherlands which was communicated to Rome requires us to consider the situation which has arisen in the country, especially in recent decades. But at the same time it can be an eye-opener in countries where this process of transformation (or, if you like, erosion) has not progressed so far. What the Dutch bishops after so many years of silence feel to be a hindrance to proclamation, evangelization or the present position of the church in society through the media affects most profoundly the broken relationship between the church leadership and the secular, secularized media in a great variety of places in the world.

Separation of church and state

The debate over the democratization of the media and media control has many perspectives, and various different lines can be singled out for development. However, a discussion of the relationship between the church and the media, which is the specific concern in the second part of this issue, cannot be carried on without some preliminary study. This includes reflection on the historicity of the mass media as cultural and social phenomena of the nineteenth and twentieth centuries.

For two centuries now it has been impossible to identify any natural harmony in the relationship between the church and an industrializing and industrialized society. The position of the church in society and in human life has ultimately been up for discussion in an increasing number of countries and among an increasing number of groups in the population. The conflicting relationships between the church and social spheres of influence led to the rise of various circuits of communication with their own structures and forms of communication. The secular and secularized communication culture is stamped by nineteenth- and twentieth-century society. The communication culture of the church became increasingly isolated and ultimately marginalized. As a result of this it did not profit, for example, from the achievements in the sphere of press freedom for which classical liberalism in the nineteenth century fought with permanent success in so many countries. Slogans like 'democratization' and 'control' or simply the lack of the latter take on another significance and specific implementation in the sphere of the public government of Western states from that in a church context. As a result the gulf between church and society becomes wider.

Democratization and control

The democratization of the mass media has at least a twofold significance. In the first place the phenomenon can be regarded as a process through which an increasing number of people participate in the messages of the communications media as recipients. Since the Industrial Revolution an increasing number of media have become available to increasing groups of people at diminishing cost. Compared with, for example, a century ago, at the end of the twentieth century there is clearly an unprecedented variety of offerings from the printed and electronic media with at the same time an unimaginably vast consumption of the media by recipients. Secondly, in the case of the democratization of the media one can think of access to the media as institutions in society, with their own form of government and a specific organizational structure. Thus the Catholic Broadcasting Company in the Netherlands is a voluntary organization with the legal form of a non-profit making association which produces non-commercial radio and television programmes within the framework of the system at a national level.

'Control' is the second key word in the title of this article, and moreover is combined with democratization. The typically Dutch form of a public broadcasting organization is also regarded inside and outside the Netherlands as 'democratic' in terms of its relationship to the authorities and other controlling spheres of influence. In this connection the American Donald R. Browne makes this relativizing comment: 'The broadcasting system in the Netherlands has often been acclaimed as a model of how broadcasting can be structured to serve society (as opposed to serving government, advertisers, media managers, the "power elite", etc.). Certainly that structure is very different from any other in the world, but there are some doubts on the part of several Dutch observers as to whether the system merits the praise it has received, or whether it will be able to adjust to changes in society and in technology.'[7]

There has never been a daily press in the Netherlands dominated by the church authorities. However, it can be said that until twenty-five years ago there was a press controlled by the church authorities, because they could nominate censors. A newspaper might call itself exclusively Catholic if the bishop of the diocese in which it appeared had appointed a priest as censor. This regulation also applied to journals. Bishops still have diocesan papers which appear weekly, fortnightly or less frequently, but the total circulation of these has declined from around 160,000 in 1986 to around 125,000 in 1992. Moreover, since Vatican II parishes have had excellent parish magazines produced by volunteers, which are valued by parishioners.[8] The very way in which these small-scale publications are edited and distributed (free for anyone who simply wants to get to know them) qualifies them as democratized and not controlled media which have a special position within church communication as a whole.

Regardless of the perspective that one chooses, the democratization of the media is a process represented by many centuries of the history of communication. Its end cannot be predicted, and probably will never come in sight, because its complete realization will always remain a utopia.

Here the difference in the degree of democratization of the media and the communication culture within society on the one hand and of the church on the other will always remain a gradual one. In human terms it seems that the church will never be able to catch up on the apparent lag. Moreover there are also examples of regressive phenomena and a marked decline in the way in which people can communicate within a particular political culture at a particular time. Freedom then turns into its opposite again.

When thinking of recent control of communication in the West one need not exclusively turn to National Socialist Germany in the period between 1933 and 1945. However, this does offer a vivid example of the loss of freedom in many areas, including that of communication. The National Socialists exercised totalitarian control and in so doing aimed at having an almost blanket effect in the spheres of both public and private, inter-personal communications. Their measures for implementing an efficient press policy and putting an effective bridle on the press affected the organization and activities of broadcasting and press concerns; it also had far-reaching economic effects and finally left its mark on the content of media messages and inter-personal conversations. What the National Socialist ideology understood by democratization defies all imagining. So-called 'people's receivers' were developed to make it possible for every household to listen to radio programmes. However, with this radio system one could receive only a limited number of stations, which could be controlled.

Expectation and reality

Press freedom is now also understood as freedom of expression and freedom of information. It belongs among what without exaggeration one may call 'the great ideas of humankind'. As press freedom is enjoyed in specific situations, determined by time and place, it is one of the essential basic conditions for the existence of societies and political systems which function in a free and democratic way. When set against 'hard' formulations in international treaties and declarations and in national basic laws and other laws, press freedom sounds idealistic: a society can strive for it with the utmost dedication, but the ideal will never be fully realized and secured for ever. Freedom of communication and control of communication constantly seem to be bound up together like Siamese twins.

Often a long period of expectation and sometimes dispute has preceded a specific concrete formulation in an article in the basic law, an international treaty or a declaration of human rights. The tension between ideal and reality usually comes to the surface the moment that attempts are made to formulate the relevant text. In that case some degree of consensus is aimed at from a situation in which there are 'as many opinions as there are heads'. After many ups and downs over around two centuries the Western countries have gone through a learning process in the sphere of freedom of the press as a legal principle and a mentality. Third World countries, the Community of Independent States (the former Soviet Union) and Eastern European countries have not been granted so much time and there are not so many phenomena of regression.

The ideal of a revolution, more especially the French Revolution of 1789 with its mythical programme of 'freedom, equality and brotherhood', underlies the Western idea of press freedom. This and other freedoms are part of the living legacy of a revolutionary verve which did not leave even the church untouched. Emancipation, belief in progress and democracy may then be rooted in the progressive tradition of the Enlightenment, but it was the French Revolution which gave them an unstoppable impetus.

In itself the myth of freedom and equality is older than the French Revolution or even the American Revolution of 1776, but this prehistory need not be discussed in the framework of the present article. It is, however, important that the *Déclaration des droits de l'homme et du citoyen* proclaimed on 26 August 1789 was drafted on North American models. The American Revolution doubtless also influenced the French Revolution at other points, but it had a different character. It was primarily the revolution of a colony against domination from the mother country. Its successful outcome ushered in the formation of the independent United States of North America, at a great distance from Europe. There the ideal of freedom and equality formed an indivisible combination over against the class-state the Ancien Régime.

Within two years, there was a break between the French revolution and the clergy. That also produced an irrevocable break between church and world. As a result Christianity lost its connections with certain modern developments. However, the church of Rome was also able to use the revolution to its advantage. In the nineteenth century it gave the impression of having learned from Napoleonic centralization. The Roman Curia built up a centralistic position of power. The church also made use of freedoms which the liberal constitutional heritage of the revolution offered it. Already in the nineteenth century the church developed a skilful approach to the question of freedom of religion. However, it feared that encouragement of press freedom and the freedom of expression which is so closely connected with it would undermine its position.

From scarcity to superfluity

Since the beginning of the other revolution, the Industrial Revolution, the Western world has been confronted with an exceptional increase in the media. The same development will take place sooner or later in the Community of Independent States (the former Soviet Union), Eastern European countries and – lagging far behind – Third World countries. The difference in stages of development, despite aid programmes from the West, is itself a stumbling block for those concerned with a fairer division of the infrastructure of world-wide communication.

In Western countries entrepreneurial productivity dominates the media. Thus newspapers and magazines are usually produced with the aim (as far as possible) of making a profit and securing the continuity of the enterprise. In some countries, including the Netherlands, in recent decades there has been talk of government support for the press and particularly for the daily papers. Remarkably enough this support has been discussed since the beginning of the 1990s, just as newspapers are encountering problems as the result of a loss of advertising income. At the same time national authorities have made possible developments in the sphere of electronic media which have had a detrimental effect on the viability of the press. The introduction of satellite broadcasting is one example of this, but one might also think of the development of regional and local broadcasting (radio and television) on a non-commercial basis.

In broadcasting, from the beginning of the commercial exploitation of radio and later also of television the United States has been dominant. Hitherto, public broadcasting has been given a very minor role there. In Europe, traditionally one or another form of non-commercial broadcasting has been dominant, usually with a high degree of government involvement. Governments have limited themselves to making rules for distributing the scarce number of frequencies. This is also thought desirable with a view to international agreements. However, this excuse for government intervention has collapsed with technological developments and in particular with the possibility of satellite and cable television. Moreover national governments expected a stimulus to economic life from less government involvement, along with permission for commercial broadcasting. In a so-called 'dual' broadcasting system, public, i.e. non-commercial, and commercial broadcasting are in competition. For guarantees of protection the public broadcasting system will remain dependent on the authorities.

In recent decades the information and communications industry has been able to profit from participation in higher education, which has been stimulated by the authorities. Teaching and studying leads to a greater demand for information from all the media. New journals have come into being for business and professions, and these have had rising circulations. An increasing use of media in leisure time has favoured the sector of public journals, in particular magazines connected with leisure interests. Anyone who does not want to read can spend more and more hours in front of the television, possibly supplemented with pre-programmed videotapes. The authorities prefer to intervene as little as possible in the content of the video medium: citizens have come of age everywhere. The age-old mechanism of the market also gives countries, even those standing outside the capitalist area, every chance to make their mark on supply and demand. This neo-liberal attitude over modern media matters is evident everywhere.

In most countries which have the character of information societies with a strong commercial element there is and has been a similar development to that in the Netherlands. In addition to non-commercial broadcasting, described as 'public', a commercial broadcasting system has developed and sometimes flourished. In structure, organization and content the media have a dynamic of their own with a tendency towards internationalization. Trans-national regulation, for example in the European Community, encourages cross-border media activities to which technological in-novations are an urgent challenge. The increasing homogenization of the media culture is a result of this. The role of the United States in the sector of film, video and television culture is so dominant that even the European countries, which are highly developed in the media sphere, cannot avoid a certain American supremacy in this sensitive sphere of the symbolic environment which takes form and content through media messages. The presupposition is that the natural and social human environment is so influenced by this that in the literature of the communication sciences there is a good deal of discussion of the rise of a media reality. This is taken above all to consist of the audio-visual media, television in particular.

Strikingly enough, Dutch and German publishers of scientific books and journals, including distinguished specialist literature, have succeeded in spreading their wings in the international market, including the American market. However, this counterbalance in the sphere of the print media can only be temporary.

The tendencies towards diversification and concentration

The rapid expansion of broadcasting companies on a commercial basis over the last ten years is not without its danger to the development potential of the non-commercial broadcasting organizations, which are much older. The presupposition is that within a dual system there are guarantees for the continued existence of the traditional programme producers. Nevertheless, public broadcasting, above all in smaller European countries like the Netherlands and Belgium, seems to be being forced into a painful process of reorganization as a result of the rise of commercial broadcasting. The consequences of this are uncertain.

Whereas there is a progressive diversification of broadcasting stations, in the sphere of the print media a new wave of concentration seems to be taking place in the 1990s. The number of titles of both daily papers and consumer journals threatens to decline further, because commercial broadcasting is affecting the income from advertisements. At the same time readers are not prepared to pay more for their newspapers and magazines and tend to devote more time to television than to the print media. It is difficult to work out what effect the marked expansion of the audio-visual communication culture will have in the long term on the reading culture. In countries where it is legally possible, publishers are trying to invest in commercial broadcasting activities in order to be no longer exclusively dependent on the advertisers' and readers' market of newspapers and public magazines.

As a result of the development I have just outlined, churches are faced with a problem: must they be dependent on commercial broadcasting or should they try to gain a place in the control of broadcasting, on its advisory councils and its programmes? That churches and church authorities in all parts of the world already have private radio and/or television stations does not give them any experience of involvement in third-party projects. In general the church authorities are concerned to play a role in the new media developments, including those which have a commercial character. All kinds of arguments can be cited in favour of the participation of the church in initiatives in the sphere of commercial broadcasting – with choice of how this is done. A problem arises if a number of Catholics feel that the content of, for example, a particular television programme conflicts with human dignity or offends a particular group of the population.

What this involves and the lengths to which the church's involvement in programming can lead emerges in an example from the Federal Republic of Germany. There television viewers in 1991/2 were disturbed at the format and the striptease shows in 'Tutti frutti', a programme screened late on Saturday evenings by a commercial television station. Anyone who has obtained a seat as a church representative on the advisory committee of such a station because it also broadcasts religious programmes finds it difficult to understand why he or she should have some share of the responsibility. The market mechanism, which is a mark more of commercial broadcasting than of public broadcasting, encourages borderline programmes with a controversial or even offensive character. How can church representatives who are in a minority on, for example, a programme advisory committee defend themselves to those they represent? Should not such people surrender their places to other advisers if there are repeated clashes in this area?

The church's access to commercial broadcasting in the sense of sharing responsibility and obtaining broadcasting time for religious programmes raises a question which has still to be thought through adequately. Experience is indeed gained by trial and error, and in the long run even the church becomes wiser. However, it is to be doubted whether this is the right way.

The media paradox of our time

We cannot expect bishops, politicians, businessmen and others who belong to the governing élite of society to have studied communication sciences. But to an increasing degree insight is expected into the way in which the media function at the end of the twentieth century. Part of the necessary body of knowledge is, for example, the connection between the media and society. If the social context changes decisively and people look for new cultural and spiritual orientations, the media have a tendency to share in this process of change. Often in such a period of structural and mental change they even function as a catalyst.

The content of media which prompt social change clearly differs from that of media which opt to retain the familiar. In recent decades the mainstream of Western media has been concerned with the democratization of society and the assimilation, if not destruction, of hierarchical structures, both ecclesiastical and secular. Rarely is anything still regarded as a matter of course here, either by journalists or by the public that they serve.

In the 1970s there was a predominant optimism among international opinion-makers in the sphere of communication developments, inside and outside UNESCO, about the role of the media in the renewal of the face of the earth. The detachment of the church prevented it at that time from joining uncritically in this chorus of jubilation. Since the second half of the 1980s euphoria has increasingly been giving place to domination by the, progressive commercialization of the media and scepticism about the benefits that that might bring. However, were not the original expectations set too high? The media are not magic charms, but aids. Careful study should be able to indicate that progress has been made in recent decades in the form of the availability of more information to more people who through more media and media messages aimed at specific groups can take part in a more varied public debate on the constantly changing great questions of our time. Church statements in the media and church media activities have a good chance of being received favourably in the context of this positive approach. If that is so, the church is not requiring a service from third parties but is itself offering a service.

Human society constantly provides the media with new material with which to confront the public in some form. Peace, justice, a future for minorities, the stream of refugees inside and outside Europe, famine in Africa, the Gulf War: how could people know about these and other subjects without the network of modern media? We owe it to the media that we know what is going on in the world. What attitude we take to what is drawn to our attention by these media, what opinions we form on it and what action we take depends not so much on these media and media messages as on ourselves. If in this sense we are no longer affected by the flood of information, that is the media paradox of our time. And finding a solution to it is a task for people of this same time.

Translated by John Bowden

Notes

1. The text is published in the information bulletin *een-twee-een* of 5 February 1993. This bulletin is produced by the Press and Publicity Service of the Secretariat of the Roman Catholic Church in the Netherlands, Biltstraat 121, 3572 AP Utrecht, Netherlands.

2. D. McQuail, *Mass Communication Theory. An Introduction*, London, Newbury Park, Beverly Hills and New Delhi ²1987, 275f.

3. Ibid., 157.

4. M. Schmolke, in an article in the Austrian Catholic weekly *Die Furche*, quoted in G. Facius, 'Das Kreuz mit den Medien. Pastoralinstruktion*Aetatis novae* – Pferdefuss in Kleingedruckten', *Die Zeitung* 20, 1992, no. 11/12, 12.

5. For a critical reaction to the paragraph on the media in the service of the church in *Aetatis novae* see the article by the theologian H. Rolfes, 'Soziale Kommunikation und Wahrheitsverwaltung, Überlegungen zu *Aetatis novae* no. 10 über die Medien im Dienst der kirchlichen Gemeinschaft', *Communicatio Socialis* 25, 1992, no. 3, 263–75.

See also R. A. White, 'Twenty Years of Evolution in the Church's Thinking about Communications', ibid., 248–62.

6. J. B. Metz, 'Kirchliche Kommunikationskultur. Überlegungen zur Kirche in der Welt der Massenmedien', *Communicatio Socialis* 24, 1991, 247–67.

7. D. R. Browne, 'The Netherlands. Plurality with a Vengeance', in id., *Comparing Broadcast Systems. The Experiences of Six Industrialized Nations*, Ames, Iowa, 131–74: 131.

8. J. Hemels, Pfarrbrief statt Bistumsblatt', in M. Schmolke (ed.), *Kirchenpresse am Ende des Jahrtausends. Berichte aus 15 Ländern Europas und aus den Vereinigten Staaten. Festgabe für Ferdinand Oertel zur Vollendung des 65.Lebensjahres*, Paderborn 1992, 16–33.

Internationalization of the Media

William E. Biernatzki

Background

The major wire services, on which most of the world's news media depend
for their international news, are dominated by American, British and
French perspectives. American films are seen in most of the world's
cinemas, but few foreign films reach American cinema or television
screens. Satellites make international news and entertainment widely
available on the world's television channels, but most of this content is
Western.

The one-way flow of television programmes was documented in a 1983
study of sixty-nine countries.[1] Intraregional exchanges had improved
somewhat since a comparable study in 1973, and wide variations were
noted from region to region, but the one-way flow remained significant. In
a 1991 worldwide study of news coverage on a single day by the wire
services, radio, television and daily newspapers, a similar Western
emphasis was noted, but it also revealed that a very wide range of news
sources is available if editors and producers want to use them. Many of the
Asian, African and Latin American media surveyed showed greater
interest in European and North American news than in that of
neighbouring countries.[2]

Many people may regard Western dominance of the media simply as a
fact of modern life, an accident of the way the industry has developed and
of the size of the major 'markets' for media contents. But some from the
developing countries, together with some media scholars, see it as a source
of serious problems. News of the less economically developed countries
gives the false impression that they are either in a constant state of war and
turmoil or the perennial victims of natural and man-made disasters. Little
reported about them is positive. These distorted images affect decisions
made about the countries and create negative self-images among their own

people. The international mass media are condemned by their critics as agents of 'cultural imperialism', scorning indigenous cultural and moral values and overwhelming them with a flood of Western images, customs and ideology. The socio-economic elites of each country are the chief clients for Western media and become so Westernized as to be alienated from their poorer fellow countrymen. Media-rich city dwellers lose touch with the problems of the rural poor.

NWICO

To right these imbalances a 'New World Information and Communication Order' (NWICO) was demanded by the 'non-aligned movement' of developing nations. In the 1970s the chief forum for debate over NWICO was the United Nations Educational, Scientific and Cultural Organization (UNESCO), where it also received strong backing from the Communist bloc. The 'MacBride Report' on these issues, released by a UNESCO commission in 1980, aired some of the complaints but reached no consensus.[3]

The mounting debate about NWICO in the early 1980s was one reason for the withdrawal of the United States, the United Kingdom and Singapore from UNESCO in the mid-1980s.[4] By the late 1980s, trying to attract them back in, UNESCO had abandoned NWICO, and most others also gave up the struggle for it.

Some of the issues discussed in the MacBride Report remain important. But the rapid evolution of communication technologies in recent years has shifted the basis of the discussion, ameliorating some problems, making others worse and creating new ones. The World Association for Christian Communication (WACC) and other non-governmental organizations and individuals have recently tried to revive the NWICO movement.[5] But, while it avoids the initial error of centring the campaign in UNESCO, where anti-democratic forces had co-opted it, it is difficult to see how the 'grass-roots' movement now advocated can seriously affect the *status quo*.

Current situation

1. Industry structures

Despite charges of 'imperialism' and 'a will to dominate', most communication imbalances between East and West, or 'South' and 'North', appear due to uncontrolled market forces. Audiences in the West, or 'North', have been able to pay for the services of the mass media, but they will only pay for what is of interest or use to them. And, 'He who pays the piper calls the tune.' With profit for their stockholders chiefly in mind, the media in turn try to give the audience what it wants – or what it can be made to think it wants – while cutting services which are not in demand. The poorer nations must be satisfied with the crumbs which fall from the table of the affluent nations for whom the loaf was baked. They cannot effectively influence the content of an industry for which they do not pay.

Failure to produce for a truly international audience is short-sighted and neglects the need even of the paying audience for an accurate picture of the world. It is partly a result of general movements of media organizations towards 'bigness', to improve competitive ability. In some cases it is influenced by a change from ownership by individuals or families to public incorporation, where the 'bottom line' of profits to stockholders is increasingly the sole criterion of success.[6] But it does not indicate a conscious intention to dominate or ignore the Third World or malignantly to distort its image. A growing perception of increasing profitability in the Third World 'market' has caused some commercial media to begin to take more account of their international audiences.

2. Public service media

Public service media, exemplified by the shortwave World Service of the British Broadcasting Corporation (BBC), free of both excessive government controls and pressure from advertisers, may be able to do a fairly good job of representing Third World interests if they have conscientious leadership.

Unlike the BBC, most other international broadcasting services are held too tightly under government control to fill the needs of audiences in developing countries. Domestic media – kept under government control allegedly to preserve their 'public service' character – too often are mere tools of the party in power, rather than instruments of development.

3. Commercial media

Commercial services feel they owe it to their stockholders to yield the largest possible profit, but some are able to experiment. 'CNN World Report', initiated by the US-based Cable News Network (CNN) in 1989, grants free time on its satellite-distributed programme and the right to rebroadcast the whole programme to any news service, anywhere, which sends it a three-minute bulletin for unedited rebroadcasting. This has created a worldwide pool of television news originating from many countries and interpreted from their own perspectives.

CNN's regular worldwide service, 'CNN International', seen on over fifty-four million television receivers outside the United States, thus far has been suited more for an American expatriate audience than for one which is truly international. CNN says it is trying to remedy this by cutting American news to only 30%. 'CNN International' now faces a challenge from BBC's new 'World Service Television'.[7]

4. Social class and appropriate technology

All international media services cater to the elites in each country who can afford the hardware necessary to receive them and have the education to understand them. The poor majority often are not directly reached. Misguided development efforts frequently introduce technologies which the elites may want but which are not appropriate to the needs of the majority of that country's people at their current level of development.[8] Even well-intentioned projects founder when locally available expertise and resources are unequal to the task of maintaining high-tech receiving equipment scattered in remote villages.

5. Availability of sources

Most countries of any size have domestic wire services, but for international news these are usually linked with one or other of the major Western services. Inter Press Service was created in 1964 explicitly to meet Third World needs but remains small. A number of regional news exchange pools have been tried, but many have failed. However, many feature services and news releases supplement news from agencies and pools. Thus, editors and producers theoretically can draw from many international sources. Inevitably, however, the news goes through a selection process. Wire service editors must decide what to use and what to 'spike', and so must local editors.

6. The fax machine

Fax machines have recently added a new dimension to the circulation of information. They have become almost a necessity in most businesses of any size, even in the developing world. Unlike computer networks, they can be used by anyone, without special training, for the worldwide dissemination of information, including news. In theory, anyone with access to a fax machine, domestic news sources, a list of collaborators around the world with similar equipment and sources, and a moderate amount of money to pay the telephone bills, can now operate a small worldwide news pool as effective as the big wire services.

7. Cinema

Hollywood films continue to dominate the world's cinema, and remain a major target for charges of 'cultural imperialism'.[9] A domestically profitable American film can be circulated more cheaply in foreign markets than films from countries with less lucrative domestic markets. Their fast-paced action and polished production techniques make US films more attractive than their competitors to audiences around the world. Although foreign interests now own the major American studios, writers, themes and settings remain largely American, and the actors and directors predominantly American and British, as they always have been. 'Cultural imperialism' may still be alive and well in Hollywood, but the 'imperialist' now is not America but a small group of transnational corporate owners.

8. VCRs

The number of homes in the world with video cassette recorders (VCRs) totalled 228,140,000, or 33.7% of the households with television in 1991.[10] The transborder flow of cassettes is almost impossible for any nation to control, and piracy, too, is rampant. The latest foreign films, including pornography, can be found on cassettes in countries which legally exclude or strictly limit their importation.[11] VCR ownership is surprisingly high in many poorer countries, especially if domestic television is limited in variety and quality.

Key problems

A big corporation is not necessarily a bad corporation, but the growing concentration of mass media ownership in the hands of transnational corporations raises concern. As stock corporations they are preoccupied with increasing stockholder profits, paying little attention to public service or disinterested innovation. They also tend to base themselves wherever the legal climate is more suited to unrestricted worldwide operations, and they are not responsible to any international regulatory authority.

The availability of media reproduction and redistribution technologies makes effective supervision of media reception virtually impossible. This facilitates political and artistic freedom, but parents' ability to supervise their children's viewing and listening is compromised. The technologies also facilitate the theft of copyrighted materials.

The reality of the 'threat' to local cultures from international media has been seriously questioned. Foreign programmes and films tend to be displaced if quality domestic programmes are available.[12] But this presumes a steady improvement in production skills and general programming quality which may be difficult to achieve in many countries.

Although the effects of advertising are difficult to chart, it can encourage consumerism and material expectations beyond the means of poor countries. Some products, such as cigarettes, are actually harmful. But campaigns against foreign cigarette advertising in some countries would be more credible if, at the same time, their media were not advertising the equally deadly products of their own government tobacco monopolies.

Prospects for the future

There is a kernel of truth for international communication in the hyperbolic claim that education can solve the world's problems. The most successfully developing countries invariably have well-educated populations. Only nations with near-universal primary education and substantial numbers receiving secondary and higher education can hope to free themselves from communication dependency. A world-wide competitive free-market system now seems inevitable, and a nation which has not taken the trouble to educate its people can never hope to compete successfully.

Education is also needed to develop a corps of creative people who can produce attractive mass media products incorporating their culture's values. At first many will copy foreign themes and production methods, but as experience and confidence grow, and with support from their own governments and other domestic institutions, they eventually can provide the culturally appropriate media which audiences will prefer to foreign imports.

Nevertheless, the Western training received by the pioneers of a non-Western country's media development will inevitably root some Western values and ideas of 'professionalism', 'news', etc., in its media culture. As regional and domestic training opportunities become available this will diminish, but it can never be entirely avoided – even were such avoidance clearly desirable.

Although a certain homogenization of forms and values can be expected to be a permanent feature of the world's mass media, unifying forces are opposed by diversifying tendencies. The ability of the mass media to create a 'global village' is a myth, or at best an oversimplification. The mass media of many non-Western countries tomorrow may come to look like that of

Japan today: international forms of technology and production conveying contents perhaps superficially Western but retaining many indigenous qualities and values.

Concentration of unregulated media ownership is as much a danger to media integrity in the developed countries as it is in the developing countries. The establishment of an independent international authority with enforcement power over transnational corporations is most unlikely, as is effective action by national governments. About all that can be hoped for is alertness on the part of non-governmental watchdogs to point out developing concentrations of media power and to lobby for inter-governmental action to limit them.

The same watchdogs might promote more balanced media flows by persuading idealists in government to act through legislation or executive authority. Another approach might be to help communications enterprises to see profit-making possibilities in establishing a truly balanced international flow of telecommunications and mass media. The first approach depends much on personalities, and so is highly problematic. The second is hindered by the stance of total confrontation many leaders of non-governmental movements seem to feel compelled to take towards the transnational corporations.

Notes

1. Tapio Varis, 'The International Flow of Television Programmes', *Journal of Communication* 34/1, Winter 1984, 143–52.

2. Rex Malik and Karen Anderson, 'The Global News Agenda Survey: Part 1', *InterMedia* 20/1, 1992, 8–71; and 'The Global News Agenda Survey: Part 2', *InterMedia* 20/2, 1992, 10–28.

3. Sean MacBride, el al., *Many Voices, One World*, Paris 1980.

4. A more important reason for the withdrawal was UNESCO's general pattern of anti-Western policies and waste of resources by the organization. Continuing rampant maladministration in the United Nations in general was documented in a four-part series of articles in the *Washington Post* in September 1992.

5. Michael Traber and Kaarle Nordenstreng (eds.), *Few Voices, Many Worlds: Towards a Media Reform Movement*, London 1992.

6. Joseph Turow, 'The Organizational Underpinnings of Contemporary Media Conglomerates', *Communication Research* 19/6, December 1992, 682–704.

7. Philip Robinson, 'CNN Set for World Battle with BBC', *The Times*, 29 December 1992, 32.

8. Gerald Sussman and John A. Lent (eds.), *Transnational Communications: Wiring the Third World*, Newbury Park 1991.

9. Emile G. McAnany and Kenton T. Wilkinson, 'From Cultural Imperialists to

Takeover Victims? Questions on Hollywood's Buyouts From the Critical Tradition', *Communication Research* 19/6, December 1992, 724–48.

   10. 'Statistical Analysis: World Video Recorder Market Reaches Maturity', *Screen Digest*, June 1992, 132–3.

   11. Douglas A. Boyd, 'VCRs in Developing Countries: An Arab Case Study', *Media Development* 32/1, 1985, 6.

   12. Michael Tracey, 'Popular Culture and the Economics of Global Television', *InterMedia* 16/2, 1988, 22–4.

Eastern Europe: The Media in Transition

Miklós Tomka

The media, more than anything else, bring into focus the transition in Eastern Europe. Their situation and role reflect political, cultural and technological changes. These differ from country to country. So the first question to ask is whether we can talk about Central Europe as a region at all. There are numerous differentiating factors: whether the tradition was that of the Byzantine or the Western church; whether industrialization has already taken place or is still delayed; the degree of urbanization or modernization. However, we cannot go into matters of detail here. My starting point is that common structural characteristics can be indicated in four spheres. These are: the transition of the media from being the centralized propaganda apparatus of the state party to being a differentiated independent system; the unchanged function of the media in social integration; the discovery of religion by the media, but treated in an ignorant and distorted way; and finally the internal weakness and contradictoriness of the specialized religious and church media. Despite individual examples to the contrary, I shall attempt to cover the whole region in the sketch which follows.

1. Media systems in political change

Short-sighted observers attribute the collapse of the Soviet empire to the politics of Gorbachev. His role in the peaceful management of the change should not be belittled. However, the causes go deeper, and are to be sought in the social struggle for autonomy, and the economy. Here mass communication played quite a considerable role. The concern for socio-economic decentralization led to the rise and reinforcement of local and regional media and were accelerated by these media. Whereas formerly an overflow could be limited to frontier areas, at the latest by the middle of the 1980s satellite programmes and the possibilities of direct reception finally broke through the cultural barriers. The spread of the video-recorder, like the rise of the cassette market which could not be controlled by the government, then finally did away with dependence on programmes produced by the state. The breach in the dam could no longer be mended. The cultural bosses of some countries continued to oppose any change in the style and content of their media with an ostrich-type strategy, and thus contributed to a shift of audience to Western programmes. In other countries the pressure of unavoidable competition led to a gradual liberalization and commercialization of the media. In both instances the attractiveness of media consumption rose.

The change of political system can be regarded as a seal on the development indicated above. Mass communication can no longer be completely centralized. There are no more monopolies. Variety in newspapers and a rise in readership go hand in hand. Only when usable frequencies put limits to competition, i.e. in the sphere of the electronic media, are there delays in differentiation. That makes it all the more natural to conclude that the media, especially in the cultural and symbolic sphere, are among the most important vehicles of democratization in Eastern Europe and faithfully reflect the structure and the power-relationships of a particular society. There are two reasons for the inadequacy of this assumption: the relative durability of the media sector and the existence of external influences.

Durability here means three things. First, the starting point in decades of indoctrination. Indoctrination establishes as matters of course statements and concepts which have nothing to do with reality and the truth. Such a cultural pattern shapes the thoughts of journalists as well as those on the receiving end of the media. So Communism lives on in people's heads. Secondly, this same ideologized culture lives on in all the products of the past: in books, films, posters, plays, and so on. Cultural politics was part of the exercising of power and therefore paid any price to disseminate its products as cheaply and in as large quantities as possible. This past cannot be obliterated. And there are no short-term means of balancing out the one-sidedness of the products of the culture of the past system. So Communism lives on in school books, in libraries, in film archives, in posters which have been left up. Thirdly, the guild of journalists cannot be changed. Journalists furthered change in many countries. But in general it can be stated that the Communist state took a great deal of trouble to see that journalists toed the line in their training, their qualification and their professional activity. Perhaps no other group was subjected to such strict selection and control. Journalists became the representatives of a quite special perspective, but were not brought up to be the sensitive recipients of social and cultural stimuli. And they became a special group with their own political and cultural interests. Their independence over against the state leadership and the Party is not uninteresting, nor is the increase in the prestige of the media which went with this. Equally significant, however, are their constant links with the liberals and the left-wing parties.

The free development of a balanced spectrum of media is also hampered by three further factors. The first is the lack of capital. Internal capital in private hands is not independent of the former party elite. The second factor is the increasing domination of the market by Western press empires. So the change is partly determined by the past and partly from abroad. The third factor is the legal uncertainty, the lack of contemporary law relating to the media, the absence of consensus over balance in the media, the insufficient control of the media through society. This could make the media a great political force, governed by economic success and the interests of those behind them: not a reflection but an independent participant in social and political processes.

2. The function of the media in social integration

The fashionable description of the social situation in Eastern Europe emphasizes the lack of a civil society. The totalitarian state destroyed all self-governing organs of society, all associations, organizations, movements and assemblies which could serve as both a link and a buffer between the individual and the state and through their own functioning relieve both individuals and the state of burdens. There is no intermediate social structure. The political order of Communism was experienced as pressure without sufficient structures to order it. This ordering of power was all too often arbitrary. People felt limited, powerless and insecure. This lawlessness in the most comprehensive sense of the word, this anomia, characterized the personal dimension of life under Communism.

The final phase of Communism could be experienced in some places as being like the atmosphere of the plague as described by Camus in his novel. People shut themselves up in their own small world and avoided others as far as possible. That time is now past. But individualism has not been overcome. Depending on the economic hopes, Eastern European societies in our day can be compared with operations during a gold rush or with chaotic mining work after an earthquake which is not quite over. Destruction and rebuilding can be found side by side. But what is predominant is the lack of morality and restraint which cannot be held in check even by a tyrant. This everyday experience, like the lack of civil society and anomia, calls for ordering principles and structures.

The collapse of Communism was a victory of centrifugal forces over the rusty ring of a basically primitive centralism. In some countries the system's loss of power and authority could even be traced by opinion polls. Information was even available about what social institutions could maintain or increase their prestige and from which society could expect stability and help towards integration. There were two: the churches and – with significant differences depending on the country – the media.

Religion in public media

Apart from occasional diversions into the criticism of religion, the media of the Communist period deleted religion from their repertoire. This has suddenly changed. Religion has been discovered as an area of public interest. After a long abstinence society now wants to be informed regularly on religious questions. No medium can afford to ignore this wish. However, how it is met is another question.

Reference has already been made to the cultural damage done by Communist indoctrination. This emerges particularly clearly in the sphere of religion. The former, terribly frivolous, criticism of religion, along with the systematic avoidance of religion as a topic, are now bringing forth fruit in the conceptual confusion of journalists, and the journalists are coming up against equal ignorance among most recipients. Instead of reporting on religion and the church, the media are constructing the topic of religion for themselves.

All too often religion is reduced to the sphere of the church and the political dimension. The interest and the understanding of the media are largely responsible for the fact that at present religion and the churches are becoming topics in a quite unique way: because of their possessions and claims to possessions, because of their political and cultural role, because of the dispute over confessional institutions, and so on. The tenacious efforts at reconstruction by the churches (and the religious groups and organizations and the orders) are interpreted as an illegitimate invasion of the public sphere, as attempts to take over political power.

Presumably it is a fundamental characteristic of the media that they portray the world in a pointed way. Perhaps the media are little inclined to communicate a solid and well-balanced basic knowledge. But what happens if, as in the case of religion, there is no basic knowledge? One solution is to exaggerate the conflicts. Now if this tendency applies to the media generally, in the post-Communist period it becomes oppressive. Interests did indeed clash in the change of social system. Under the pressure of the situation, representatives of the church were in fact compelled to take part in political and other negotiations without sufficient knowledge of the matter, and as a result much china was smashed. There are plenty of conflicts. But the picture goes wrong if religion and the churches are seen only from this perspective.

The politicizing of religion and the description of it in terms of conflict go along with an increasing sharpness in criticism of religion and the churches. For decades religion was said, sometimes by the selfsame journalists, to be a private matter. Its public presence is now seen by many as fundamentally illegitimate. Different concepts of religion, different notions of society collide. The liberal understanding feels directly challenged. Its repudiation of Communism took place in a pragmatic context. However, its argument for a world built on factual laws is an attempt to impose the symbolic power of the expert. The existence of an institution concerned with world-view and morality is a limitation on this claim. Criticism of religion and the churches is partly rooted in group interests.

4. Religious media

The specialized religious media are a significant special case. For forty years they were severely restricted in most Eastern European countries. The new era has led everywhere to the rise of a broad range of new papers and programmes. At least three factors within the churches largely determine development. First, the religious part of society is not among the major consumers of culture. People have lost the habit of looking for religious education. One often comes across an anti-intellectualism with spiritualistic trimmings. Although church people are getting younger and the number of Christian academics is increasing, the market for the religious media, especially the serious media, is oppressively small. A lack of demand and the undertow of commercialization are difficult to overcome.

Secondly, there are at most isolated links and intermediate stages between the religious and the secular media. Apart from this, the religious media are organs for a limited, closed public. They use a language of their own and order topics in a way which corresponds to church expectations, but which does not encourage acceptance outside the church or lure people out of the isolation of the religious ghetto.

Thirdly, structural tensions in the church also burden the media sector. The disputed question is how the inner division in the church can be healed. The intellectuals argue for free speech and for the brotherhood and sisterhood which arises out of dialogue. They hope for a combination of unity and multiplicity. Another solution would be integration even in the churches' secular links under hierarchical leadership, the restoration of the pre-conciliar form of the institution, which would then make individual trial and error and testing unnecessary and lay down the rules for communication. The former strategy tends to be put forward by lay people, the latter by the clergy. The impossibility of reconciling them at present makes a third position necessary: religious life in a narrow circle without the possibility of – perhaps even dispensing with – more comprehensive communication. This polarization confronts the media at any rate with the choice whether they will decide for one of the options already mentioned or whether they will strive to mediate. However they decide, they must expect criticism and conflicts. The division of the church must first be suffered and endured in the particular context before there can be any healing.

5. Open questions

In the process of reshaping the church some fundamental decisions must be taken, and the media can play a part in preparing for them and implementing them. Probabably the most important question is whether the churches in Eastern Europe can summon up the courage and strength for a dialogue with the world or whether they will persist in a monologue. Will they understand the worldliness of the world as a gift of God? Can they recognize the Christian content of secularization? Will they accept the minority situation of believers as an opportunity and a task? Will they be able to affirm the plurality, the provisional character, the modernity of our world and accept it as a sphere for realizing the kingdom of God? On the answers depend whether the religious media are given the role of propagandists dependent on the church or whether they can be the vehicles of an authentic dialogue.

A second question concerns the capacity of the media for mediation. Splits in organization, the long period underground, the lack of a church public, very different access to foreign sources, created widespread time-lags in different parts of the churches of Eastern Europe. Some followed the spirit of Pius XII, others that of John XXIII. The reception of Vatican II still lies in the future. How can this 'cultural lag' be worked through? The question is whether a public can be created within the church, despite the time-warps in the basis for dialogue. And finally, there is the issue how the difference between the worlds and perspective of the clergy and the laity can be, if not abolished, at least relativized by a common framework. This challenge also affects the media.

The third question is whether the media can link the churches of Eastern Europe with the world church and remind them of their global responsibility. The Iron Curtain could be destroyed, but a lack of understanding still continues to divide. The compulsory second language in this sphere was Russian. The reception of Western ideas frequently comes up against language barriers. In addition there is the difference in cultural development. In the East there are often complaints about the decadence and neo-paganism of the West. Quite a number of church people are afraid of being infected by Western ideas. People avoid contacts of a non-material kind. barriers to communication are preferred to dialogue. Perhaps even more suspicious is the blind spot to all Third World questions. The churches of Eastern Europe – perhaps with the exception of Poland – have yet to perceive the unity and solidarity of all humankind and the whole earth. Global responsibility is an alien term. Can the religious media change anything here? Can they establish communication beyond their own tribal area? These are open questions! And the media themselves are part of the churches which are seeking a way.

Translated by John Bowden

II · The Church and the Media

The Electronic Trap. Theological Remarks on Televised Worship

Johann Baptist Metz

The editors of this issue of *Concilium* have asked me to repeat some remarks made recently at an international congress on the media about a church culture of communication in the age of the mass media, and to concentrate on the question of presenting liturgical services on television.[1] I am glad to do so, not because my critical reservations have diminished in the meantime, but rather because they have increased – in particular over the state of our television world.

Two extreme positions

Two extreme positions can be detected in characterizations and assessments of the mass media, especially television. Putting it simply, one position presupposes that the medium determines the content ('the message'). Here we have media theories which take up Marshall McLuhan's 'the medium is the message', for example those of J. Meyrowitz, N. Postman and, in the German language area (contrary to earlier remarks) of H. M. Enzensberger with his characterization of television as a zero medium. J. Baudrillard's criticism of simulating reason can be regarded as a sociological radicalization of this theory about the media. Again putting it simply, the opposite position represents the view that the content ('the message') determines the medium; here the medium remains a completely innocent medium, has a purely catalytic effect, and is regarded as a neutral instrument of communication. This understanding of the medium seems to me to persist in church statements on the issue:

there is already an example of this in the 1971 pastoral instruction *Communio et Progressio* on the instruments of social communication (published in the wake of the Second Vatican Council – completely in line with the understanding of technology which governs *Gaudium et spes*).

It was probably this 'naive' theory of the medium which (in Germany at any rate) encouraged the trend towards the private media. As long as it's under our control, the dominant view was, nothing can really go wrong. For it is not the instrument of communication which determines 'the message', but only the communicator and his intentions. Since then it has become increasingly clear what we get in such a situation: not a 'good programme', in the sense of proclamation, but a 'well-meant' programme, and that is quite the opposite of a good programme. In my view, in the private media in particular it is becoming increasingly clear how much all information is drawn into the undertow of entertainment, and how much every programme is drawn into the undertow of advertising.

Social communication: yes, but . . .

Here I would prefer to adopt a 'middle' position, which takes television seriously as an instrument of information and social communication, and therefore expects it to provide audio-visual reports with pastoral relevance. However, here we should not forget that this instrument of information and social communication can at the same time work as an instrument of social and cultural deprivation. This ambiguity becomes evident above all in the effects of television on the so-called Third World. Even in our Western world, people talk of the dangers of a new, secondary dependence, a secondary illiteracy, which is being produced and encouraged by the mass media. And how are things in the Third World, among the poor countries of this earth? Do not the time-lags in the process of modernization have a particularly drastic effect there? In these countries it is by no means primarily religion which is the opium of the poor. Today, it seems to me, it is mass-media culture which in the meantime has forced its way into the poorest houses. It lures the unfortunate people into an imaginary world of consumption and success. It alienates the poor from their own language before it has finally made them culturally literate; it robs them of their memory before they have become aware of their history of suffering; it makes them weary of themselves as subjects before they have become the subjects of a free world. This modernization of the head by modern television culture produces an imaginary consciousness, a kind of loss of perception of reality. And this has an effect at the lowest level of life, as the only dream and comfort which is still available. 'Among us,' remarked a Brazilian expert on the media, 'television is a great supermarket which supplies imaginary goods to the poor.'

The broadcast of worship – no!

However the possibilities of social communication by television may be assessed, this communication is of very limited use, if any, in the broadcast of worship, i.e. cultic communication. In other words, whatever else may be broadcast, at any rate the sacramental centre of the liturgy, the celebration of the eucharist, does not belong on television!

In the 1950s, when television spread through Europe, for a while there was a vigorous discussion as to whether the Mass should be broadcast on television, in other words whether the television camera should show and offer to everyone what faithful Christians who physically join in the celebration of the mystery of the church may and do see. For a long time this discussion has fallen silent. The question now seems to have been decided clearly. As early as 1971, the pastoral instruction cited above summed it up like this: 'The broadcasting of the holy mass certainly belongs in religious programmes (on television) . . .' (no. 151). Certainly? Karl Rahner was one of those who joined in this early discussion. At that time he was strictly against the mass on television.[2] In his view the complete and full celebration of the eucharist is a preferred object of that metaphysical reserve which prohibits making this event accessible to a random, scattered and uncommitted public. In my view, what has been offered since then on 'electronic religion' is the most massive violation of this metaphysical reserve.

A new 'arcane discipline'?

Like Dietrich Bonhoeffer before him – 'the unbeliever also has access to the word, but not to the sacrament' (1937) – Karl Rahner recalled an old church tradition, the 'arcane discipline'. As is well known, this was a kind of obligation to secrecy, a specific ban on making something public, which in early Christianity above all applied to the celebration of the eucharist in the pagan environment of the time. It then more or less disappeared, from the fifth century on, when there were no longer any pagans or unbelievers. Granted, both the origin and the motivation of this early Christian arcane discipline remain ambivalent; so it could not be repeated without it being suspiciously anachronistic. But that does not mean that any form of Christian arcane discipline can be dismissed with the remark that 'in principle the doctrine and worship of Christians are public'.[3] The question arises here, in particular for a theology which is critical of society, what public is meant. Certainly the eucharist is not completely without a public character. But does not the specific television public, which does not (and cannot) define itself in terms of 'salvation' and 'holiness', exclude the eucharist? And not only the eucharist? Whole worlds of language are excluded by the typical (and perhaps unavoidable) language of television presenters. Both progressive and conservative criticisms of culture converge in referring to the corruption of the public in the mass media. Thus for example Walter Jens recently remarked in connection with the experience of private commercial television: 'We no longer have a medium which creates a public; we no longer have a healthy provocation but the cynical destruction of the foundations of a society which has at least some solidarity.'[4] And for Botho Strauss the publicity provided by television 'brings together and modulates the most contradictory frequencies – in a tumult of understanding'.[5]

Anyone who insists on a new arcane discipline here; anyone who calls for restraint in communication; anyone who does not want to expose worship here to the osmotic pressure of a constantly changing world of images; anyone who does not want to mix up the *memoria passionis* with the language of television presenters, is not evading the issue of publicity but criticizing it. Such people are insisting on a remnant of metaphysical reserve in cultic praxis.

A basic admonition

Here the general practice covered by church statements is much less concerned. It knows no tendency to a new arcane discipline in our world, dominated as it is by the mass media. But the medium itself requires the utmost attention. Walter Benjamin with his famous thesis on works of art already knew this.[6] One could already learn from this that two constitutive elements of the world of worship are lost by the reproductive media: first authenticity, because the medium abolishes the difference between original and copy; and secondly the tradition, because the reproductive medium robs its content of connections in time and space. Reproduction takes the place of tradition, i.e. it occupies this space. Authenticity and tradition can only be saved, if at all, by physical participation.

The motivations for church praxis in the media

What has moved the church to give up its reservations over the broadcast of worship? Even secular society knows about data protection; it seems that the church no longer has such protection for its secrets. How could it come about that the church does not make sufficient distinction between a participatory public at the celebration of the mystery and the reproductive publicizing of that mystery in a strictly egalitarian mass culture? What is the church doing by making its central cultic celebration public on the mass media? Does it want to 'advertise' or 'evangelize' with the centre of its liturgy? Is it anxious that otherwise it will not be sufficiently present? Should it not rather be afraid of the virtually fatal effect of television on material in making it hackneyed? And does it not know that the more inescapable and indeed almost omnipresent the media become for us, the more stimulating and attractive will something be one day which does not appear on them and cannot be seen on them.

One point which keeps being made is that the eucharist, and worship generally, is on television above all for the sick, the old and the lonely. That seems to be pastorally conclusive. Nevertheless, I have my doubts here as well. I learned from my mother that part of growing old in faith is that one learns to accept no longer being able to 'be there'; that one learns to do without being together at worship; and that for those who are old and sick another 'sacramental event' is particularly important, the 'sacrament of brothers and sisters': personal communication, personal visits to the old and sick. Sometimes I suspect that electronics are increasingly intended to replace the personal encounter and communication that the old and sick need as part of their pastoral care.

So has not the church, which is otherwise being so hesitant in modernizing itself, fallen into a trap of technical modernization by broadcasting the mass on television? And is it not time for the church to free itself from this?

Translated by John Bowden

Notes

1. Cf. J. B. Metz, 'Kirchliche Kommunikationskultur. Überlegungen zur Kirche in der Welt der Massenmedien', *Communicatio Socialis* 24, 1991, 3/4; shorter version, 'Was ist mit der Gottesrede geschehen?', *Herder Korrespondenz*, September 1991.

2. Cf. K. Rahner, 'Messe und Fernsehen', in *Sendung und Gnade*, Innsbruck 1959, 187–200.

3. As e.g. can be read in the 'Guidelines for the Broadcast of Liturgical Services on the Media' (produced by the Internationale Arbeitsgemeinschaft der Liturgischen Kommissionen im deutschen Sprachgebiet 1989) against the appeal to a new arcane discipline.

4. *Die Zeit*, 10/1993.

5. *Der Spiegel*, 6/1993.

6. W. Benjamin, 'Das Kunstwerk im Zeitalter seiner technischen Reproduzierbarkeit' (first and second versions), in *Gesammelte Schriften* I.2, Frankfurt 1974.

The Church and the Mass Media[1]

Gregory Baum

Since the Vatican Council, the Catholic church has adopted an open attitude towards the secular culture in which it lives. Catholics believe that the God revealed in Jesus Christ is opeative in the whole of human history, in the lives of individual people, in their cultural achievements, their social struggles and their political efforts to build a just society. This openness produced a new respect for the world. According to the conciliar document *Gaudium et spes*, the church must communicate its message to the culture in which it lives in the idiom of that culture, that is to say using the ideas and the terminology understood in that culture. *Gaudium et spes* (no. 44) called this 'the law of all evangelization'.

Communication of the good news

This conciliar theology generated a new approach to communication. The church's conversation with the society in which it lives demands that the church find appropriate symbols, metaphors and languages to make its message heard. But what is the church's message? All agree that the gospel of forgiveness and new life is not confined to the religious dimension narrowly defined, but includes an ethical summons and a vision of society. The New Testament announces God's approaching reign. This reign becomes manifest as God overcomes our cynicism by faith, our despair by hope, our hostility by love, our indifference by solidarity, and our violence by peace. The gospel imperatives are not 'strangers' to society, since they are honoured by many people who do not call themselves Christian. At the same time, paradoxically, these imperatives are 'strangers' to society defined by its dominant structures.

This paradox deserves attention. I shall call the two contrasting ways of understanding God's presence in the world 'liberal' and 'radical'. Liberal

Christians emphasize that gospel values are not 'strange' in the world. These Christians have a hopeful view of society. They see God's presence in the freedoms of individuals: the freedom to follow their own conscience, the freedom brought by democracy, equal opportunity and free enterprise, and the freedom of people to strive for personal authenticity. These freedoms, we note, are also appreciated by secular liberals.

Radical Christians, by contrast, hold a more Augustinian view of society. They hold that gospel values are 'strangers' in the world. Radical Christians share with secular radicals a keen awareness of the contradictions of society: they focus on the global economic system that organizes the world's resources in a brutally unjust and environmentally destructive way. They denounce the dominant class culture that trivializes the present crisis, legitimates the existing system and persuades people that nothing can be done to transform it.

For Christian radicals, God is present in the world first of all as judgment: God declares the world to be sinful. Yet the God of judgment is also the God of new life. For radical Christians this new life is present in the people who stand against injustice and seek to overcome it. While liberal Christians are struck by the 'similarities' between gospel and modern culture, radical Christians are struck by the 'difference'; they search instead for 'similarities' in the counter-culture produced by society's critics.

Both the liberal and the radical perspectives have great strength. But since they also have their weakness, it is important that liberals and radicals remain in dialogue. The weakness of liberals is to believe that good will and personal virtue suffice to make society more just, while the weakness of radicals is to be so impressed by the force of the dominant structures that they underestimate the power of individuals to make a difference.

The distinction between 'liberal' and 'radical' is helpful for understanding the church's task of communicating its message in the idiom, concepts and terminology of modern society. Should these be taken from the cultural mainstream, as liberals suppose? Or should they be taken from the critics of society and the struggle of the marginalized, as the radicals suppose? This question cannot be answered in a general way. Christians have to debate this issue in their own cultural context. They have to decide, for instance, what attitude the church should take to the mass media and whether the church can use them to communicate its message.

The critique of the mass media

The mass media of communication are an exciting development at the heart of modern society. They embody human intelligence, artistic talent and technological innovation. They exercise great power in shaping contemporary culture. In North America, the culture they produce is largely defined by competitive individualism, consumer values and ethical relativism. Mass media do much more than mediate information: they create the categories in which we perceive the world. It is generally recognized today that life in the family, in the school, in business, in society and even in the churches is strongly influenced by the public media of communications.

This enormous power raises two questions for the church. First, how can the church help its members to retain their spiritual freedom in the face of this powerful cultural pressure? And secondly, can the church use the mass media to correct the dominant cultural trend and possibly even communicate its own message? The church, I wish to argue, must respond to the mass media in two ways, by 'critique' and 'intervention', that is to say by providing its members with critical skills and supporting them in their effort to use the media intelligently and creatively.

Frankfurt School Critical Theory provided media criticism over fifty years ago. More recently social and literary critics with a variety of philosophical backgrounds have produced an important literature of media cricitism.[2] By decoding the media messages these studies enable people to protect themselves from being overwhelmed by these messages and to remain faithful to their own convictions. This literature tends to fit into what I have called the radical paradigm. It analyses the power of the public media to control the human mind and protect the interests of the dominant groups in society. This literature, I suggest, could help the church to formulate and communicate its own critique of the mass media.

At the same time, media criticism, even when brilliantly done, tends to suffer from the weakness of the radical paradigm: it does not appreciate the freedom of individual actors – in this case, communicators and artists working in the media – to make a difference. The critical literature creates the impression that the men and women who work in television, radio and newspapers, despite their good will and imagination, are caught in large corporate mechanisms that transmute every new vision into an ideology defending the existing order. If this were true, the intervention of Christians in the media would be useless.

'Media literacy'

Media criticism has recently been developed by an international network of educators who think that school children, from the earliest grades on, should acquire the simple skills of decoding the media messages and thus be able to learn from them and enjoy them without being brainwashed by them. These educators call this approach 'media literacy'. Media literacy programmes have been introduced in the school systems of Australia, England, Scotland, and, a few years ago, in the Province of Ontario, Canada. The Ontario Ministry of Education has produced a book entitled *Media Literacy*, a guide for the teachers who communicate the critical skills to their classes.[3] While this book does not touch the religious issue, its approach could usefully be introduced in Catholic schools, seminaries and colleges. I wish to offer a brief presentation of the eight 'key concepts' mentioned in the book's introduction that are applied through the entire text. These key concepts are pertinent to the church's task of media criticism.

1. *All media are constructions*. 'The media do not present simple reflections of external reality: they present productions which have specific purposes. The success of their productions lies in their apparent naturalness . . . In fact, they are carefully crafted constructions that have been subjected to a broad range of determinants and decisions.' Because they are produced so well, 'it is almost impossible for us to see them as anything other than a seamless extension of reality'. The critical task is 'to expose the complexity of the media and thereby make the seams visible'. There are of course many imaginative presentations that do not pretend to reflect external reality, but they too are complex and they too have been crafted through a process that included decisions on several levels of production.

2. *The media construct reality*. 'All of us have a construct, the picture we have built up in our heads, of what the world is and how it works. It is a model based on the sense we have made of all our observations and experiences. When a major part of these observations and experiences comes to us preconstructed by the media, with attitudes, interpretations and conclusions already built in, then the media, rather than we ourselves, are constructing our reality.'

The media produce a gaze that interprets the world. This key concept helps us to understand that Christians want to use the public media not simply to offer religious information, nor necessarily to portray religious themes narrowly understood, but rather to communicate a 'gaze', a mode of interpreting the world that corresponds to the gospel.

3. *Audiences negotiate meaning in the media*. This concept reveals that in understanding the media, we are not passive receivers but make our own contribution. We bring something to the understanding of the text. We receive the communication through our own personal needs or through our social location or, more consciously, through our own critical awareness. If I am a person who was beaten and badly treated by my father and still suffer from this, I will 'read' stories dealing with children and their parents in a special way and discover in them messages other people may not see. And if I belong to a visible minority, then a special sensitivity will allow me to 'hear' certain tones in the communication that escape the majority of listeners. If I am a person consciously identified with the gospel of Jesus, I will also 'read' the story, the play, the news report or the documentary in a special way, sensitive to what we have called 'the similarity' and 'the difference' between public values and the values of the gospel. This key concept brings to light the freedom enjoyed by the reader, listener or viewer of the public media.

4. *Media have commercial implications*. 'Media literacy includes an awareness of the economic basis of mass-media production and how it impinges on the content, techniques and distribution. We should be aware that, for all practical purposes, media production is a business and must make a profit.' Students should be aware of the increasing concentration of ownership of the media in fewer and fewer hands, as well as the development of integrated ownership patterns across several media.

5. *Media contain ideological and value messages*. 'Media literacy involves an awareness of the ideological implications and value systems of media texts. All media products are advertising in some sense – for themselves, but also for values or ways of life.' The ideological messages contained in television narratives are often almost invisible because they correspond to the values written into the dominant culture. If these programmes were seen by people belonging to a different culture, their ideological messages would stand out very clearly. But for people belonging to this culture, a special intellectual effort is required to decode these programmes.

The fifth key concept opens the door to Christians and others critics of society to produce texts, programmes and stories that question the dominant values and propose an alternative.

6. *Media have social and political implications*. 'An important dimension of media literacy is an awareness of the broad range of social and political effects stemming from the media.' The media have an impact on the changing nature of family life and the use of leisure time and recreation. The mass communication of popular culture often becomes the matrix within

which young people define their relationship to one another and to society. The media often determine the manner in which people become involved in political issues at home and in the problems and needs of other countries.

7. *Form and content are closely related in the media.* The thesis of Marshall McLuhan that 'the medium is the message' may be an exaggeration, but it points to the important fact that the form of the communication contains its own style and grammar and hence codifies reality in a unique way. This correlation is the reason why Christians have asked themselves whether the mass media are capable of communicating the gospel message. Do the media transform the sacred into the secular? After many hesitations the Catholic church finally decided to support the efforts to communicate the Christian message through the public media. But the problem remains.

8. *Each medium has a unique aesthetic form.* Decoding and understanding media texts is not enough. Media literacy should also help students to enjoy the beauty, the pleasing forms and effects associated with different media. The artistic dimension of communication deserves to be appreciated fully. This key concept opens the door to the creativity of the communicator and the artist working in the media.

Media intervention

The eight key concepts mentioned above do not say very much to enhance the power and freedom of the communicator to intervene and make a difference. Still, the key concepts included three references that could be expanded. The first has to do with the broad range of determinants and decisions that enter into the carefully crafted construction of the message. Here intervention is possible. For the communicator with a vision or gaze at odds with the mainstream, for instance the Christian, may well be in a position to influence decisions regarding media policy, programmes and contents. Secondly, the key concepts brought out that the media contain value messages and thus have social and political consequences. Here again intervention is possible. It is possible to produce texts and programmes that reflect gospel values and promote justice and care in society. Here is room for creativity. And thirdly, the key concepts include a reference to the realm of the aesthetic. Media are powerful because they are pleasing: sometimes they simply entertain us, sometimes they delight us because they portray what is beautiful, sometimes they move us deeply because they communicate through signs and symbols an understanding that transcends ideas and concepts. The exciting field of media production, calling for art and creativity, is a space for intervention.

The key concepts mentioned above do not refer to religion at all. What religious media productions want to communicate, we note, is not only a critique of society and the social values of love, justice and peace, but also – simultaneously – an inkling of the sacred. God is love, justice and peace, but God is also always the other, the different, the transcendent, whose love, justice and peace surpasses our own concepts and imagination. Is it possible to communicate religious experience through the public media? Can a radio or television programme lead us to a moment when the narrow perspective on life opens up, when we perceive the deeper truths we hold but do not attend to, when we are touched by a gentle power that comes upon us as redemption and new life? I think so.

This issue takes us back to the above-mentioned 'law of all evan-gelization', i.e. the church's commission to communicate the good news in the idiom of the culture in which it dwells. But what is the idiom of contemporary culture? Radical Christians are tempted to argue that the stories and symbols of present-day culture are all marked by an ideology of domination. When they are used in religious communication, the radicals will say, they tend to reconcile people with society as it is and hence exercise an ideological function.

I wish to argue that radicals should resist such a sweeping judgment. Here the liberal Christian perspective becomes important: God is always already at work among people, even before the word of the church reaches them. The present culture is made up of many different layers and trends, some of which express the redemptive dramas of human existence, the healing of the broken, the release from imprisonment, the passage from darkness to light, the joy over an unexpected and unmerited gift, the resurrection from the dead. Here God is graciously present. These dramas exist among us: they do not reflect the way of the world, they rescue us from the world. These dramas, like the gospel itself, have a paradoxical quality: they are both 'strangers' and 'not strangers' in modern society. Because God is present in the struggles of human life and in the human effort to articulate them, I hold that Christian artists and communicators are able to communicate the gospel in the idiom of contemporary culture.

Notes

1. This article is the edited version of an address given at the congress of the Canadian 'office national de communications sociales' at Cap Rouge, Quebec, 4 June 1992.

2. Theodore Adorno, *The Culture Industry: Selected Essays on Mass Culture*, ed. J. M. Bernstein, London 1991; *Media, Culture and Society: A Critical Reader*, ed. R. Collins, London 1986; Nicholas Garnham, *Capitalism and Communication*, London 1990; Daniel Miller, *Material Culture and Mass Consumption*, New York 1987; Raymond Williams, *The Sociology of Culture*, New York 1982.

3. Media Literacy: Resource Guide, Ministry of Education, Government of Ontario, Queen's Park, Toronto, Canada 1989.

Church Documents and the Media

Paul A. Soukup

The church, particularly the Roman Catholic church, has seldom hesitated to speak out about communication and the means of communication. Indeed, Baragli's collection of church documents on communication lists some 755 statements from the time of Gutenberg (1464) until 1973.[1] In the more recent past, since the Second Vatican Council, the Catholic church has issued three major conciliar or post-conciliar documents, almost thirty papal 'World Communications Day' messages, various papal addresses to groups of communication professionals, two papal encyclicals that indirectly address communication concerns, a dozen or so statements by conferences of bishops, another dozen or so major letters by individual bishops, and countless episcopal 'Communication Day' messages. Among ecumenical groups, the World Council of Churches and its constituent organizations periodically publish declarations on communication; associations such as the US-based National Council of Churches of Christ regularly distribute instructions or statements as well.

On the whole these documents tend to address serious issues in a fairly competent manner. They fail where they try to do too much and where they choose confusing approaches and limited methods of analysis.

This review commentary will not consider the 'occasional' statements (annual messages, addresses and so on) because, by definition, they depend on particular circumstances; focussing principally on policy documents instead, it will describe their background and content and evaluate their treatment of issues. Chief documents included in this review are *Inter Mirifica*, *Communio et Progressio*, *Aetatis Novae*, *Evangelii Nuntiandi*, *Redemptoris Missio*, the World Council of Churches' Uppsala and Vancouver statements, and the US National Council of Churches of Christ's paper, 'Global Communication for

Justice'.[2] Following Jorgenson[3] we will ask: Who issued the statement? Which audience does the statement address? What is its purpose? What are the issues it raises?

Inter Mirifica

At the end of its second session in December 1963, the Second Vatican Council promulgated *Inter Mirifica*, a relatively short statement on communication. In it the leadership of the Catholic church called on people of good will, civil leaders, Christians and Catholic communicators to recognize the church's interest in and right to use what it terms 'the means of social communication'. (Although these include the press, the cinema, radio and television, and the theatre, the Council prefers not to use the more common English 'mass media' because the latter term misses the social dimension of the former.) *Inter Mirifica* makes two principal claims: that the use of communication media should follow the moral order and that church members should place communication media at the service of the apostolate.

However, in the issues it addresses, the conciliar document goes much farther than these claims. First, it shifts away from the narrow, reactive approach to communication that characterized earlier Vatican statements. Second, reasoning from the moral order, the nature of communication, and the nature of human societies, it asserts people's right to information (no. 5); it recognizes the importance of public opinion (no. 8); it balances the rights of artistic expression with the demands of the moral order (nos. 6–7); and it divides moral responsibility for communication between producers and recipients (no. 9–11). Third, it calls for a much more active church involvement with all means of communication: supporting 'worthwhile' periodicals and programming (no. 14), training priests and laity to work in and with the media (no. 15), developing media education in Catholic schools (no. 16), urging greater financial support for church efforts (no. 17), and establishing an infrastructure of communication offices from the local to international levels (no. 18–22).

Communio et Progressio

Recognizing its own limitations in this technical area, the Council also called for a more developed pastoral instruction on communication. In January 1971, the Pontifical Commission for the Instruments of Social Communication published *Communio et Progressio*, the Catholic church's longest and most detailed treatment of communication and communication media. Like *Inter Mirifica*, it addresses all people of good will as well as Catholics. The communication specialists who prepared the document planned it as a careful exposition of the church's position on communication, with a two-fold grounding: first, in a doctrinal discussion of a Christian view of communication, and second, in a formal analysis of the role of communication in human society.

With this background, *Communio et Progressio* develops many of the issues posed in *Inter Mirifica* and introduces a number of others, particularly in reference to the church itself. In the doctrinal section (nos. 6–18), the document lays the groundwork for a theological approach to communication, finding in the doctrines of the Trinity, creation and incarnation a basis for a distinctly Christian view of communication. From its thematic statement that communication exists to serve the unity and advancement of people living in society, it develops a strong claim for freedom of public opinion (nos. 24–32); it establishes the right to be informed and to inform – including freedom of speech, access to the means of communication, and the right to communicate (nos. 33–47); it encourages educational and cultural uses of mass communication, justifying the autonomy of artistic expression while noting that artists face moral problems when they portray evil (nos. 48–58); and it offers some guidelines for advertising (nos. 59–62). *Communio et Progressio* echoes *Inter Mirifica*'s call for education and training for both producers and recipients of communication; it grounds its appeal in the need to develop human qualities, to serve others, to strive for justice, and to become better members of society (nos. 65, 72). The pastoral instruction also stresses the issue of dialogue as fundamentally important to society – both producers and recipients must actively seek to increase dialogue with each other and within society (nos. 73, 81). Finally, *Communio et Progressio* asks for co-operation. In one of its few appeals to civil authority, the document calls for co-operation between citizens and governments, noting that government has a positive role – not to censor but to guarantee free speech, free expression of communicative initiatives, and free exercise of religion (nos. 84–91). National governments should work together for communication and development, particularly in the emerging nations. All peoples should similarly work together for communication that serves human dignity and human progress.

When it turns its attention specifically to the church, *Communio et Progressio* raises a number of new issues and gives detail to some traditional ones. Most importantly, the instruction applies its conclusions regarding public opinion and dialogue to the church itself. Because communication and dialogue are essential to strengthening the bonds of union in the church, 'Catholics should be fully aware of the real freedom to speak their minds which stems from a "feeling for the faith" and from love' (no. 116). Similarly, church officials should foster public opinion within the church (no. 117), taking care that doctrine is not confused with matters of opinion (no. 118). Local churches are asked to provide pastoral care for communication professionals, co-operation in reporting news about the church, theological reflection on communication, media education programmes, and communication programmes as part of pastoral training in seminaries (nos. 102–12). The church, both universal and local, is invited to make greater use of the media in evangelization and education, paying particular attention to quality (nos. 126–34). Catholics working in each sector of the communication industry – the printed word, the cinema, radio and television, and the theatre – receive words of support and advice. *Communio et Progressio* concludes with a very practical section addressing the needs for equipment, trained personnel, and professional organizations for Catholic communication.

Aetatis Novae

Issued by the Pontifical Council for Social Communications to mark the twentieth anniversary of *Communio et Progressio*, *Aetatis Novae* reiterates many of the themes already outlined. However, the document seems narrower in scope, on the one hand addressing only the church or church communicators and, on the other, failing adequately to ground its claims or fully to describe the changed context of communication (on which it bases its recommendations). It does deal with matters of some importance: the economic domination of international communication by a few transnational corporations (no. 5), the effects of the communication industry on local cultures (no. 16), the defence of the right to communicate (nos. 14–15), and the church's own ministry to form and offer pastoral care to communicators (nos. 18–19). One new element is an insistence on the urgency of pastoral planning for communication in each diocese or region; indeed, *Aetatis Novae* goes so far as to include a lengthy appendix outlining such a pastoral plan: vision statement; inventory of media environment; structure for church communications; media education; pastoral outreach to media professionals; financing; links with Catholic education at all levels; spiritual formation; theological reflection; co-operation with religious congregations, ecumenical organizations and secular media; public relations; research in local and national communication needs; and support for public interest communication programmes, ethical standards, access to media, and development communication (nos. 23–33).

Encyclicals

Two papal encyclicals mention mass communication in a direct way. Both encyclicals address themselves to the church about its missionary mandate and activity. Paul VI, writing in *Evangelii Nuntiandi* in 1976, repeats the theme of church utilization of the media from *Inter Mirifica* and *Communio et Progressio*: 'The Church would feel guilty before the Lord if she did not utilize these powerful means of communication that human skill is daily rendering more perfect' (no. 45). John Paul II breaks new ground in his 1991 encyclical, *Redemptoris Missio*, by calling for church understanding of the media context rather than only for church use of mass media. The church's missionary outreach, he writes, includes cultural sectors – the chief of these being the world of communication – as well as territories (no. 37). John Paul II's letter offers a much deeper insight into the social role of communication than any of the earlier documents; it also integrates communication much more closely into the larger pastoral activity of the church.

Ecumenical documents

The World Council of Churches has included communication and the mass media in its assembly reports from 1954 to 1983,[4] sometimes noting only in passing their importance, particularly in their forms of inter-personal communication, witness and public relations. The reports from Uppsala and Vancouver differ, though, in that they devote special sections to mass media.[5] The first half of the Uppsala report (1968) provides a background study of the mass media: their impact in daily life, their social functions, their socio-economic roles and their impact on the church. The document continues with a theological reflection on the interconnectedness of communication, community, revelation, Incarnation and Trinity. On this basis, the report concludes: 'this means that not only the use, but also the structure and the function of the media require the full involvement of the Christian community' (p. 395). The report raises questions about the structures of domination and power enshrined in the media and their need for a liberation and salvation modelled on the *kenosis* of Christ. The report ends with recommendations that the church learn more about communication issues; that it support the free flow of information; that it co-operate with other groups to promote public interest policies, artistic quality in productions, and more just ownership policies; that it support equitable use of satellites; that it work to ensure economically poor nations access to information; and that it train people for special ministries in the mass media.

The Vancouver declaration (1983) takes quite a different form. Written not by communication experts but by the delegates to the Assembly, it reflects anxiety and puzzlement about the new media as well as the hope that the communication experience of the assembly itself – a human encounter in a 'market place of experience and conviction' – might characterize all communication. Balancing positive and negative elements of the mass media with an awareness of their inherent injustices, the group supports the demand of the South for a New World Information and Communication Order. Credibility, not media power, should characterize church communication. Such credibility takes into account intention (affirm people and respect cultural differences), content (build justice and promote wholeness), style, dialogue, appropriateness, mystery (respect the 'otherness' of the gospel), and value reversal. The declaration ends with a recommendation that the church seek credibility through dialogue, through experimenting with alternative forms of communication, through media awareness programmes, and through integrating communication in theological training programmes.

In 1992 the US National Council of Churches of Christ issued a challenge for justice in communication.[6] Noting concentration of ownership, market needs ascendant over cultural or national needs, and the elimination of global dialogue on the one hand; and communication as God's gift, the role of communication in glorifying God, liberating and creating community, and the necessity of prophetic Christian communication on the other,[7] the group calls on its member communions to take a strong advocacy role to reform communication policies. Among the strategies it urges on the churches are media literacy programmes; the integration of peace, justice and advocacy agendas for global communication; support for more news coverage of developing nations; support for satellite spectrum space for developing nations; support for the voices of oppressed persons; and the affirmation of the right of all people to their own styles of communication, advertising, and entertainment.

Evaluation

Although church documents on the media address a commendable range of important issues with some insight, they also suffer limitations stemming from their own inconsistency of approach, confusion of audience, and methodological choices. Jorgenson[8] has pointed out that church documents broadly take an authoritative or a provocative approach and that the media documents tend to combine the tactics. After reviewing the set of documents here, one might add that they also mix analytic and didactic approaches. Granted that one might have a provocative analysis or an authoritative teaching, this combination still leads to some confusion. Is a given statement meant to describe a situation neutrally or to provoke a response? Does a particular appraisal or call for action carry any moral weight to obligate its readers? How seriously and in what fashion does the church take these statements? Clearly, what provokes thought differs substantially from what binds the conscience. Because virtually all of the communication documents fail to distinguish among these possibilities, the reader comes away from them with mixed feelings. This ambivalence may also result from an uncertainty in regard to audience, particularly in the Vatican statements. At different times these address all people of good will, civil leaders, all Christians, all Catholics, and Catholics in the media. How one accepts the analysis or counsel may well depend upon which group demands one's allegiance.

The more serious weaknesses in the documents result from their methodology. First, they seldom distinguish among forms of communication. All consciously choose to discuss mass media (the press, radio, television, the cinema, the theatre) but nevertheless refer to alternative media (traditional or folk forms and small-group media such as slides or cassettes) and to dialogue and interpersonal communication. Each of these bears an analogical similarity to the others, but their striking differences demand a more careful analysis. Second, the documents tend to take the mass media on their own terms, accepting current social-science findings. This leads to a kind of optimistic or idealized view of these media which sees them in instrumental terms and not as social structures.[9] Thus any critique tends to focus on symptoms rather than on underlying causes. Third, each document makes a number of moral claims about the mass media (ranging from the need to regulate programme content to guaranteeing the right to communicate to the necessity of protecting Third World access). These claims often rest on different intellectual and theological foundations which are not clarified and are sometimes misapplied, as happens, for example, when a model based on conversational dialogue or on an incarnational theology grounds a claim about television. Fourth, the documents simultaneously address both the broad question of the mass media and the narrower concern of the church's use of those media. This latter question involves not a little self-interest on the part of the church. Whenever it arises, it raises some doubts about the impartiality with which the church has criticized the media.

The final weakness of these documents may or may not stem from them but is amply documented in their texts. Few in the church seem to pay them any attention. The same directives occur with a kind of sad regularity.

On balance, though, the church documents on the media reward a careful reading. for the most part they are competently prepared and they certainly highlight many important issues. Their best value lies in their being read as starting points for further discussion and action rather than as conclusions.

Notes

1. E. Baragli, *Comunicazione Comunione e Chiesa*, Rome 1973.

2. Important among the documents not considered here are the communication sections of the Latin American Bishops' Conference statements from Medellín (1968) and Puebla (1979), the Swiss Churches' sixteen propositions on the media (1983), the Lutheran World Federation's 'Facing the Communication Revolution' (1982), the Administrative Board of the US Catholic Conference's statement *In the Sight of All* (1986), and the pastoral letters on communication by Milan's Cardinal Carlo Maria Martini (*Effata, Aperti*, 1990, and *Il Lembo del Mantello*, 1991). Other documents, principally from Catholic European sources but including some ecumenical materials, can be found in Médiathec (ed.), *Les Médias: Textes des Églises*, Paris 1990.

3. L. Jorgenson, 'Church Statements on Communication: Their Place in a Process', *Media Development* 31.1, 1984, 30–2.

4. These are the reports of the Second Assembly (Evanston, 1954), Third Assembly (New Delhi, 1961), Fourth Assembly (Uppsala, 1968), Fifth Assembly (Nairobi, 1975), and Sixth Assembly (Vancouver, 1983). The Seventh Assembly (Canberra, 1991) did not directly address communication or media, although in the preparatory materials, issue 4 of subtheme 2 was titled 'The Challenge of Communication for Liberation'.

5. World Council of Churches, *The Church and the Media of Mass Communication*, Geneva 1968; D. Gill (ed.), *Gathered for Life: Official Report, VI Assembly, World Council of Churches, Vancouver, Canada, 1983*, Geneva 1983.

6. Intermedia Department, National Council of Churches of Christ, *Global Communication for Justice*, New York 1992.

7. These characteristics of Christian communication are taken from the World

Association of Christian Communication, *Christian Principles of Communication*, London 1990.

8. Ibid., 30.

9. C. Hamelink, *Perspectives for Public Communication: A Study of the Churches' Participation in Public Communication*, Baarn 1975.

How the Churches Deal with the Media

Ottmar Fuchs

I. The kingdom of God as a theological point of reference

Ecclesiologically, the positive theological point of reference for the relationship between the church and the media (like any relationship of the church to its own environment) is given by the fact that the church responsibly indicates the initial realization of the kingdom of God in history: in word and action, in proclamation and diaconia, in symbols of transcendence and in actions of love for neighbour. However, this realization of the kingdom of God is not limited to the church, just as there is much in the church which has little to do with the kingdom of God. In its actual presence, what on the basis of revelation the church can call the kingdom of God, giving hope and encouragement, transcends the church – not only in the actions of love and justice performed by many people, but also in many religious and non-religious symbolizations, in so far as they maintain hope in situations where there is little hope, and put the options of justice, freedom and love into practice even in situations where there is a threat of meaninglessness and also risk.

A basic question about the future of the church is how it determines and shapes its relationship to the kingdom of God outside itself, and how honestly and courageously it tackles that within it which is incompatible with love of God and neighbour. Any black-and-white contrast between 'inside' and 'outside' leads to the ghettoizing of the church and prevents an inculturation on the basis of an exchange with all forces of good will which is both theologically possible and necessary.[1] The more Christians and church social forms deal disinterestedly (in terms of maintaining their institutions and recruiting for them) with other men and women and spheres of life, the more convincing, inviting and attractive they will be for seekers. Offers of this kind of experience and aids towards orientation which are then no longer open to the suspicion of indoctrination and recruitment will play their part in encouraging interest in the church among people who have come of age.

The time of 'all-or-nothing' pastoral work is finally over. Perhaps we should really learn from that pastoral work which is increasingly possible and necessary in the major cities,[2] the 'pastoralia of the passer-by'. To the degree that the churches represent themselves and their concerns in the form of 'personal offers' at various central places of human life and experience, in the meditation in a city church, in an hour's conversation with someone who may then go away again, in the media in high quality religious broadcasts. In all these examples it is no longer possible to calculate what is 'coming out' of them and who is 'returning'. What the church authorities are understandably fond of defining as pastoral success, namely the degree to which their own work also makes some contribution to their own organizations (from church attendance to active presence in key communities) may need to be qualified and supplemented by another attitude: any increase in hope and humanity which is made possible and advanced by religious and church initiatives is through and through a work of the kingdom of God in this world (even if those addressed do not come into the inner sphere of the church) and thus falls essentially under the responsibility of the church. Like the kingdom of God, so too the pastoral work of the kingdom of God points far beyond the maintaining of its 'own shop'.

This also relativizes the question, so constantly raised, of the meaningfulness of church broadcasts on the media, whether they reach those who are remote from the church and whether they serve to bring the audience back into the church. Much more important is the question of whether broadcasts sponsored by the churches take such a form that those who have become distanced are reached in such a way that their *own* capacity for hope and humanity is built up; in other words, if they feel, 'Here we aren't being got at, but something is being given to us.' To use a church symbol: here they are being given bread for life (and not sweets, to attract them).

II. Forms of religious presence in secular products

The question of religion in the media prompts the question: which religion? For religions, too (measured by their power to humanize and heal), are completely ambivalent entities. In the name of religion people can build one another up and destroy one another. Human nature can be confirmed and legitimated to a gigantic degree with the concept of God, but so too can its shadow side. We know such experiences not least from the history of Christianity. We must not lose sight of this ambivalence even in the various manifestations of Christianity on the media.

The explicitly religious element in secular productions

First I want to discuss secular entertainment products in which religion appears in one form or another (comes off well or badly), not least also because such religious components even have entertainment value for the public and serve as a form of identification. I am thinking on the whole of non-religious (i.e. 'secular') broadcasts with religious settings, i.e. with language and content that one knows from the church. Sometimes the curiosity and entertainment value of religious worlds is so great that whole series are devoted to them – for example soap operas are constructed round the figure of a pastor.

Let's look at such a secular religious programme in more detail. I remember a scene in Ingmar Bergman's film *The Serpent's Egg* (1976). The film is set in Berlin at the height of the inflation of late autumn 1923. Anxiety about violence and about the future dominate's people's feelings. Against this background Bergman sets a 'religious' scene which at the same time is one of the most human images of this film, indeed of any film that I know. Manuella goes into the sacristy to an elderly priest after mass: she feels or knows that she is guilty over the suicide of her husband, whom she had left. At first the priest turns her away (he has to get on with the next service as quickly as possible), but then he starts a conversation with her in the sacristy and feels her deep spiritual need. When he suggests that they say a prayer, they both kneel down. She asks, 'Is it a special prayer?' 'Yes, yes, yes, be quiet,' and after a pause he continues, 'We live so far from God that he probably cannot hear us when we ask for help. So we must grant each other the forgiveness that a distant God fails to give.' Then he puts his hand on her head and says, 'The death of your husband is forgiven you; you need no longer feel guilty.' After a pause he continues, 'I ask your forgiveness for being so remote, so forbidding; please forgive me.' Somewhat amazed, she looks up, now puts her hand on his head and says, 'Yes, I forgive you.' 'We cannot do more,' says the priest, breaking off the conversation quickly to get away as soon as possible, so as not to offend his superior.

So in the midst of this bad time, when already (like the reptile in the transparent serpent's egg) the monster of later National Socialism is visibly incubating, this utterly inter-personal encounter of reconciliation in the sphere of religion, for all its brokenness, and a faith which in the face of what people are doing to each other can 'experience' God only as the one who is utterly remote, but nevertheless holds to him, can give content to that inter-personal reconciliation with its silence. In this broken situation the unbroken assertion of the nearness of God would only have seemed inhuman, and the expedient of a church official. But not only are these words impressive; so is the combination of them with the attitude and the faces of the pair. The priest also kneels, and both individual's eyes show pain and liberation at the same time.

  This pentitential scene offers a welcome contrast to quite a number of films in which 'the church' and 'the clergy' do not come out well: because as functionaries of the church powers they are blind to human needs, because they act on the side of the rulers, because they treat non-believers in an inhuman way, because they cannot cope with the sexual-erotic dimension of love or, if they can, because they do so only with a secret dual morality. Even if the increasingly naive and brash clichés of such productions, which in part are despising of the church and in part are just trivial, get on my nerves, it cannot be disputed that there too, partly in an apt way and partly in caricature, religious reality is disclosed, in its perverse manifestation which is so humanly destructive. Proud defensive and injured retorts are not much use here, where we are talking (like the confessor mentioned above who kneels and asks for forgiveness) about where religion itself has been and is guilty.

Implicit Christianity in secular products

  But there are also secular productions which do not translate religious and Christian concerns into religious language and forms of communication (or in negative instances get in their way and destroy them), but adopt as it were an anonymous, yet nevertheless realistic, approach. This happens when (in positive instances) the option of humanity and justice, of mercy and reconciliation, is put forward or dramatized in a series of images (for example in reports or scenes which draw attention to social problems, in films and series in which solidarity, tolerance and conflict is lived out).

  From a theological perspective, anything that strengthens and builds up mercy and justice between human beings has to do with the praxis of the kingdom of God.[3] Here the Christian criticism of the media has the same task as Christian proclamation to contemporaries who are remote from *diakonia*, namely to appreciate their action and to learn from them for its own praxis. In our world there is more expression and realization of humanity than talk of God. If churches and pastorates and their sphere of influence are not to turn into the opposite of this, they must pay attention to this practical 'strange prophecy' which can provide stimulation for imagining possibilities of realizing the kingdom of God outside themselves.[4]

The presence of the church in the media

In these two forms of the presence of religion in the media it is not the church which uses the media as a means of expression for its concerns. Here it is those responsible for the media themselves who explicitly or implicitly include religion and Christian elements in their secular broadcasts. More attention will be paid to such forms of the presence of religion in the media if the media are not used as instruments for church interests but there is co-operation with those who work as producers and artists in a way which builds up relationships that bring mutual recognition and enrichment. I would argue emphatically not only that the presence of Christian content in the media should be seen and organized from the perspective of church initiatives and institutions but that a structure of encounter should be built up which is as constructive as it is critical (on both sides) – one which is not active on behalf of the church and perhaps also 'outside' it, but one which is intrinsically connected with what the church calls the kingdom of God. If this is clear, then it may also be said that the church has a right to be represented in the media and to put forward its own concerns.

So there are the quite explicitly religious broadcasts which are predominantly made by the church editors in broadcasting organizations. They arise from within the churches and in their interest (structurally this also applies to broadcasts which are critical of the churches). Here the level of interest can be very different depending on the area: from rulings by the church authorities to the free work of Christian journalists. The public for such material probably consists largely of church insiders and to a lesser degree of those who are neither close nor distanced, those who are still interested and already distanced, and to a very small degree those who are remote from the church – here the nature of a broadcast and its imagery can also address the latter to an increasing degree. Research into individual instances will have to clarify how much this is then the case.[5]

Church broadcasts can also be divided into two groups: programmes explicitly concerned with proclamation, the assurance of faith (like the German programme 'Wort zum Sonntag') and the symbolic communication of the content of faith (Sunday mass on television), and programmes in which the praxis of Christians and congregations – and also their activities in society and the world – are looked at in order to bring them into a positive or critical connection with the values of the gospel (explicitly, or simply because a particular broadcast takes place in the affirmative context of a church radio station). One example might be the presentation of a social initiative in which Christians and those remote for the church act together for people in need or those suffering under injustice.

III. Learning to hear and see

The topic of how the church deals with the media relates to two large groups of people: the many who work in the media, who produce and are responsible for broadcasts, and all those who hear and see the results of this work on radio and television. Whereas so far we have been particularly concerned with how the church authorities deal with the media, with what aims they produce them and how they relate to non-church products and producers like artists, now we shall be mainly concerned with the question how the public deal with the media, how they become competent critics of the media and where the criteria for this competent criticism come from.

This aspect of the church's use of the media is often overlooked. But the church has a social and ecclesial responsibility not only for its own appearances on the media but also for seeing that those who receive the media are not manipulated and belittled, but find that the media strengthen their powers of being and communicating themselves. In that case we are not just dealing with professionals who represent the church on the media but with church people as the subject of dealing with the media. In other words, we are dealing with how the churches as the people of God use the media.

What in particular can the social resources of church communities do so that people are not presented with all kinds of information and entertainment together with the value orientations which are more or less explicitly conveyed in them, and in addition presupposing every possible kind of religion, but rather are offered help in distinguishing between what is useful and what is damaging, between what is un-Christian and what is Christian? It is the task not only of media pedagogics but also of pastoral work, in order to help Christians to come of age (and this is a theological option according to the Vatican II theology of vocation), to encourage the active creativity of the viewer in church and society.

Accordingly, it is necessary for people to be able to classify the products of the media in terms of importance. The apparatus, the professionalism and the technical perfection of media products suggests (as does the printed word in the sphere of books) an objective general validity which transcends the individual, which these media cannot have because in each case they are always human products that are no more and no less valuable and can no more or no less be valid than their recipients. The solution is not to stop reading or looking at the television but to be able to relativize the significance and scope of such products in the same way as the material of interpersonal communication. As audiovisual messages usually have a much more marked emotional impact on the psyche than what is read or heard, this postulate applies above all to television and videos. Make no mistake about it, this is not because they are worse (certainly there is also a lot of bad printed matter), but because even if they are bad, they can be very effective (above all where there is a combination of sex and crime).[6]

There is a real danger that people do not take their own 'direct' experiences as seriously as the 'secondary'[7] media experiences. The empirically demonstrable contradictions between public opinion and everyday experience brought out by sociology are illuminating in this context: whereas marriage and the family are losing significance in public opinion as expressed by the media, in questionnaires the generally positive experience of families and a high opinion of them come through almost intact. The public assessment of divorce as a relatively trivial matter contrasts with the general experience of depression among divorced persons (including their constant longing for a successful partnership and in part also for a family). 'Many people mistrust their own experiences and values and do not think that they can be capable of generalization, although they are demonstrably shared by the majority.'[8] In such a double climate of opinion with its split between personal experience and public assessment, people evidently find it difficult to assert their own individual experiences over against the images communicated by the media. Here in fact something like a public marginalization of important personal experiences takes place.

IV. Not flight, but 'walking upright'

The media have become a source of everyday experience which can no longer be unthought. There are hardly any spheres now which are free of the media unless one goes into an anachronistic ghetto, and in that case one also cuts oneself off from links with the central processes of exchange in present-day society. Furthermore, a general defamation of those active in the media, which is inherent in this reaction, does not do justice either to these people or to their product.

Nor is a black-and-white ideologization of 'secondary' experiences over against 'primary' experiences tenable; it distorts the insight that the former can be very constructive and the latter very destructive. There is no unambivalent sphere of human life, society and the media which does not have both negative and positive possibilities. However, it is important for the public to have some self-awareness, to regard as important and real what does not appear on the media, and also to promote values which are passed over by the media. Conversely, I can well remember excellent programmes which (for example by broadening horizons) point to charitable and political needs and in so doing identify values which have been lacking in everyday public awareness.

In short, what needs to be done is to break down hierarchical relationships and to build up relations of parity between the different subjects and institutions in society.[9] Of course this is a question of power, not just socio-political and structural enabling but also of that psychological enabling which has made the various social forms flourish for individuals. This insight immediately raises a question within the churches: are our congregations such that people in them can develop strong selves and empower themselves? Are they communities in which adults are questioned about their creativity, their personal faith and their practical activity?

How important it is to strengthen people against the influences of the mass media also emerges in families which have problems of communicating because the television has not just become an additional 'member of the family' but in fact is the dominant one.[10] Here it is no use church representatives accusing families of a lack of Christian socialization if at the same time the social forms of the church do not help to strengthen and build up what is important to parents for *their own* faith and life, for example enabling them to open their mouths in the community even when they are going against the stream, without the inconvenience that they cause being punished by pressure to fall into line or by expulsion from the community. Parents are relatively helpless over their growing children unless they can learn to speak about their own faith (and their own doubts). For young people will hardly be convinced about the faith with mere formulae of assent and catechism answers. It is better if they can experience identity here, and perhaps also honest questioning and helplessness, from their parents. But if that is to happen, parents must first have learned to deal honestly with themselves and their own weaknesses in encountering others and God.

A meaningful and effective pastoralia of the media will aim at two goals: a lowering of quantity (in consumption of the media) and an increase in quality: media economy and media coming of age. The two are connected: for where time and energy are taken up with all too much media consumption there can no longer be any mature reactions, because these need time for reflection and discussion.

V. Economy and coming of age

If the capacity to keep a distance and select from what one encounters is a function of human coming of age, then it is vital to call for a reduction in the flood of images, so that concentration and the investment of time in a good film is again possible. The danger in the excessive amount of audiovisual material that is on offer is not that it wastes time but that it wastes energy. That there should also be some social time in addition to working time and media consumption time should be a very important concern for the culture of family, community and social encounter. For social time is that time in which we are primarily involved in taking up and cultivating social relationships and the social forms that go with them, which have value in themselves.[11]

For believers, the concept of social time also has another dimension, that of encounter with God. Where there is no time for resting, for solitude and for prayer, spiritual interruptions of the everyday hardly have a chance. 'Prayer is resistance to the banality which threatens our lives, to the total focussing of our life on a society of exchanges and needs.'[12] The more space is actively sought for social time, and especially time with God, the more economic and selective we shall have to be in dealing with the media. This does not exclude the possibility that the mass media can also communicate encounters with God, for example in broadcast meditations, in conversations, services and so on, but these will always be surrounded with more sensational and more spectacular material, unless we have already learned in the sphere outside the media to long for the more peaceful image and the capacity to see behind it.

Here it becomes clear how much the church not only does a service to society but also makes possible its own proclamation of God when it develops alternative forms of shaping leisure time in family and community: for example in groups in which people meet regularly that cut right across stages of life or specialist interests, to discuss particular broadcasts or films and exchange views about them, possibly also for a time of rest and reflection, in order to experience and encourage their own creativity and competence.

The detachment and criticism which are made possible in communicative forms of reception also leads to the discovery and development of a sense of detail, a feeling for the small and unobtrusive features that are to be found in the background of good media productions. Productions will be linked with human experiences and need not be consumed privately at home and remain undiscussed (as they often are in the family). In the community work often connected with this the first and important attempts at a community-orientated media association are being made in the parishes.

Initiatives could increasingly be connected with this in which a community's own products made with whatever media means are available (above all by video), either local documentaries or plays, could be produced and discussed. Here it would be an advantage for the churches to learn from alternative political and social video groups and associations how 'proclamation from below' might be possible in the media. It is at such interfaces between technical media material and its use in spheres of dialogue encounter that citizens and Christians who have come of age will make some decisions for the future (of the politics of both the media and the church). For the 'domestication' of media techniques and products from the context of the mass media in interpersonal encounter gives an experience of dealing with the media which can then also have some effect on the wider reception of the mass media. Church institutions and forms of community are increasingly resorting to such a network of media and personal communication, in theological faculties, in adult education, community work, and the various specialist groups and age ranges, and in the connections between them.

Translated by John Bowden

Notes

1. Cf. in detail O. Fuchs, 'Kirche und Medien auf den Weg zum Jahr 2000. Anmerkungen zu einem römischen Textentwurf', *Stimmen der Zeit* 106, 1991, 411–21.

2. Cf. W. Simon, *Kirche in der Stadt*, Berlin 1990.

3. Cf. O. Fuchs, *Heilen und Befreien. Der Dienst am Nächsten als Ernstfall von Kirche und Pastoral*, Düsseldorf 1990.

4. Dorothee Sölle has developed the concept of 'realization' for defining the theological relationship between secular literature and its religious and Christian content: 'Realization is the secular concretion of what is "given" or promised in the language of religion', and 'Theology and literature here stand in the relationship of tradition and concretization, of promise and realization', *Realisation. Studien zum Verhältnis von Theologie und Dichtung nach der Aufklärung*, Darmstadt und Neuwied 1973, 29, 48.

5. Cf. H. Bogensberger, 'Das Publikum kirchlicher Medienverbund-Programme', *Diakonia* 17, 1986, 6, 422–4.

6. Cf. M. Kundczik, *Gewalt und Medien*, Cologne 1987.

7. For the possibility and problems of this term cf. O. Fuchs, *Kirche – Kabel – Kapital. Standpunkte einer christlichen Medienpolitik*, Münster 1989, 108–14.

8. R. Köcher, 'Familie und Gesellschaft', in E. Noelle-Neumann and R. Köcher, *Die verletzte Nation. Über den Versuch der Deutschen, ihren Charakter zu verändern*, Stuttgart 1987, 83.

9. Cf. in more detail Fuchs, *Kirche* (n. 7), 152–70, 192–217.

10. Cf. R. Merkert, 'Der Bildschirm als Familienmitglied', *Communicatio Socialis* 15, 1982, 3, 167–92; Köcher, 'Familie' (n. 8), 77–8.

11. Cf. P. Spescha, *Arbeit – Freizeit – Sozialzeit*, Frankfurt am Main 1981.

12. J. B. Metz (and K. Rahner), *Ermütigung zum Gebet*, Freiburg im Breisgau 1977, 35.

The Bishops and Abortion: A Case Study in Reporting Church News

Michael A. Russo

In April 1990, the American Catholic bishops hired a leading public relations firm, Hill and Knowlton, to advise them on a forthcoming anti-abortion campaign. Despite the initial public furore over this, the motives that brought the bishops to hire professional media counsel simply acknowledged what many insiders have long known. Namely, church leaders must consider how the church communicates publicly about abortion and a range of other internal and external issues. This implies a recognition of the curious phenomenon that the 'world' includes Catholics who largely get their religious news from the secular media of press, television and radio. Consequently, the church cannot escape this aspect of modernity.

At the same time, observers of press performance such as the *New York Times* writer Jason DeParle believe that much of the abortion coverage has not been especially good when it considers morally complex issues and, according to David Shaw of the *Los Angeles Times*, reporting has been biassed in favour of abortion rights.[1] The abortion story is complex and does not fit into neat journalistic categories. If the press, and the media generally, identify themselves as having the role of stimulating this great public conversation, the challenge to our democracy becomes how the press, television and radio report about and seriously consider issues of public morality in a language that advances our moral and political lives. We must remind ourselves constantly that though the church is essentially spiritual, and the press secular, neither can neglect the implications of the moral.

In this article, I consider key features of the press coverage of abortion in the United States and the roles of three Roman Catholic ordinaries,

Cardinal Joseph L. Bernardin of Chicago, Cardinal John J. O'Connor of New York and Archbishop Rembert G. Weakland, OSB, of Milwaukee. In writing about Bernardin, O'Connor and Weakland, I am struck by the fact that as public persons, they use the media differently. Each gives voice to particular themes in the abortion debate from which to examine the church and the press. Each draws from and represents those distinct cultural voices – intellectual, organizational and political – deep within the American Catholic tradition.

I. Cardinal Bernardin and the media

Joseph Cardinal Bernardin has remained the centrist among the American hierarchy and author of the 'consistent ethic of life' approach to matters of public morality. In personality, he is kindly and resourceful. He is the architect of the structure of the NCCB/USCC. For him, process is very important. He respects the opinion of others. He seeks to build a type of 'consensus', a meeting-ground wide enough for all to stand on without shouting or rancour.

While believing 'good press' to be helpful, Bernardin has never considered the press, television or radio central to his own personal mode of communication. Perhaps he was not fully comfortable with the combative nature of the media. Instead, Bernardin has relied on his staff to help develop and filter his message to the church organization and general public. His aim was to get on the record concerning matters of public policy with few surprises.

In an interview with me, he acknowledged: 'I don't have any problems with the press. Could "good press" assist you? Well, the majority of people don't read the *New World* [the newspaper of the Chicago Archdiocese]. Rather, people are guided by television and the daily paper . . . good press can go a long way!' Concerning press conferences, he admitted: '[They] are something I have to do. It comes with the job. It's not something I like to do.'[2] Thus, in an electronic era that demands instant analysis, or 'spin', all within the time-frame of a neat 'soundbite', Bernardin is not spontaneous.

One illustration of Cardinal Bernardin's style of communication was his press conference in November 1989 at the annual meeting of the National Conference of Catholic Bishops. As the Chairman of the Bishops' Pro-Life Committee, his task was to respond to reporters' questions concerning the hotly debated abortion resolution which stated: 'No Catholic can responsibly take a "pro-choice" stand when the "choice" in question involves the taking of human life.' The floor debate among the bishops had prompted serious questions from reporters. While the text of the resolution avoided the issue of penalties, or excommunication of aggressively pro-choice Catholics, this became the subject of the press conference.

Peter Steinfels of the *New York Times* asked: 'What exactly is the meaning of the added language in the resolution . . . that "no Catholic can responsibly take a pro-choice stand"?' Bernardin replied: 'We expect politicians to act conscientiously and this seems to me to live up to a conviction you have . . . ultimately, to protect the unborn.'[3] Here Bernardin appeared unclear about how individual bishops should respond to the situation of politicians who take an aggressively pro-choice position. When further pressed by reporters about those bishops who were calling for excommunication of pro-choice politicians, Bernardin reacted by saying this was a subject for 'study'.

A year later, Bernardin, reflecting on this press conference, told me: 'The first thing the press focussed on was the questions of penalties, and really did not let up on it. And, in effect, they were saying this is the first round in an effort to begin penalizing people or excommunicating or to do whatever else. And that was not the purpose of the statement.'

In his attempts to represent the range of opinions among the bishops, Bernardin had failed to state his own position adequately and reinforced the idea that abortion was a 'Catholic' issue. This was not his intention. In hindsight, greater clarity or simply honesty in admitting that the bishops were divided over tactics would have been the better course.

My purpose here is not to expose the inadequacy of Bernardin's style with the press. Rather, I wish to show how difficult it is for anyone to represent the broad array of Catholic voices, opinions and tactics even in a circumstance where the bishops are solidly united around a specific moral teaching such as abortion. Bernardin's notion of consensus did not appear to work in terms of the tactics that some of the bishops were suggesting. Clearly the bishops were divided over tactics, and it was the press's responsibility to report this.

Bernardin and many of his fellow bishops take great care about what they say in public. Naturally, they know that once in a while they may have to say unpopular things. As Bernardin said: 'It comes with the job.' The sociologist Robert Bellah told a group of bishops recently: '[It] may be precisely the responsibility of the bishop or the priest to say things that most people do not want to hear.'[4] This requires considerable moral courage: one of speaking to moral concerns and, at the same time, of morally challenging Catholics, and even of disagreeing with large segments of the American citizenry.

II. Cardinal O'Connor and the media

John Cardinal O'Connor, the most politically vocal among the bishops, has positioned himself as the leader of the church's pro-life wing. Shortly after the announcement of his appointment as Archbishop of New York in 1983, he told reporters: 'I will use you in every way I can. I would like to be able to talk personally and individually with everyone in New York and everyone in the United States but I can't do that. So I will use you.'[5] O'Connor's intention was to extend the moral authority of his pulpit by using the mass media of television and the press to get his viewpoint across to New Yorkers and the nation.

To accommodate the media, O'Connor was available for reporters' questions each Sunday following his 10.15 Mass. His remarks on abortion and a range of topics such as hostages in Lebanon, racial incidents in the city, and heavy metal music made him a New York celebrity. The cardinal's style of communication was more spontaneous, unplanned, unrehearsed and problematic when one considers the contentious nature of New York politics. Every media war that followed – with the *New York Times* and other liberal newspapers over state abortion funding, gay and lesbian rights, pro-choice Catholics – involved a central issue: whose voice would be heard.

In an interview with Cardinal O'Connor, I asked him what he believed a newspaper or the press should aspire to. He eagerly replied: 'The truth, objectivity, the truth!' He added: 'To me the most irresponsible thing a reporter can do, or an editor, is not to do his or her homework . . . lack of professionalism . . . to take a story whatever the data are, whatever the facts are, and twist it to fit his or her preconceptions. That I suppose with the New York press corp is my most severe disappointment. I would like to see a responsible press that either ignores the story or prints the truth to the degree it came by the truth.'

In response to questions about the ideological orientations of the New York press, Cardinal O'Connor demonstrated his first-hand knowledge. He said: 'In the tabloid press, for instance, in the *Post*, and the *Daily News*, for every story that rakes me over the coals there is going to be one that praises me. I don't get a sense with those two tabloids of a philosophical hostility . . . I think that the *New York Times* has tried harder and harder to be fairer to the church. [But] they are so steeped in that abortion ideology that they're never going to get that right . . . They're never going to do a decent editorial on abortion.'

Thus, O'Connor represented an authoritarian Catholic presence challenging Catholics and other citizens alike. The New York press, in part an elite, intellectual media whose responsibilities included that of managing opinions, had its own language of 'moral discourse'. The conflict between the two forces was inevitable, and the potential for misrepresentation and distortion abounded on both sides.

In November 1989, Cardinal O'Connor replaced Cardinal Bernardin as the Chairman of the Bishops' Pro-Life Committee. By March of the following year, the central features of a national pro-life campaign began to emerge, including the hiring of Hill and Knowlton, and the Wirthlin Group, for a projected three million dollar media campaign. Ironically, the hiring of professional media counsel may have marked a turning point for John O'Connor as well. His symbiotic and sometimes impulsive relationship with the media remained his greatest problem. He, too, faced having to change. The cardinal had always believed that he could talk above the media in his own constituency in New York; now, as the chairman of the Pro-Life Committee, he had to account to his fellow bishops.

The liberal *National Catholic Reporter* echoed a common complaint: 'There's a growing annoyance among some US bishops that the New York media in general, and the New York Cardinal John O'Connor in particular, are all too frequently determining the church's public agenda.'[6] In effect, bishops around the country were in the situation of having to explain and, at times, defend O'Connor's actions and statements. Since O'Connor had so identified himself with the East Coast media, both were obvious targets. Clearly, the many combative moments between O'Connor and the media, and between O'Connor and Governor Mario Cuomo, so much the O'Connor style, had to be tempered and attuned to new political realities. This required careful planning, strong organizational skills, able staff, less spontaneity in public, and for him, the unaccustomed position of being the 'point-man' among his colleagues the bishops.

III. Archbishop Weakland and the media

Having considered the roles of Cardinals Bernardin and O'Connor, I turn now to Archbishop Rembert Weakland, because he represents another distinct voice in the church today. He is often perceived as a liberal among the bishops, and expressed his concerns about abortion and sexual morality in a series of public meetings with women in his diocese in March and April 1990. This action drew criticism from Vatican officials and leaders in the pro-life movement.

Weakland enjoys the company of journalists, and has written occasionally for the *New York Times*, *Commonweal*, and the London *Tablet*. He
is also very knowledgeable about how newspapers and journalists influence opinions and he is an occasional guest before editorial boards such
as those of *Time* and *Newsweek*. He makes a clear distinction between the
editorial policies of Milwaukee's politically liberal *Journal* and those of
the more conservative *Sentinel*. In my interview with Archbishop Weakland, he told me: 'I enjoy talking to the *Journal* editorial boards . . . The
Sentinel I find more ideological. And that's the harder group to deal
with.'[7]

Concerning abortion, Weakland spoke from the perspective of the
American political culture and noted: 'I'm inclined to think that the
church has minimized the difficulties. So the question of two values is
constantly being brought into question. The one being the value of
human life in the womb. The second being the value of choice . . . I
don't think we have thought out clearly the relationship there between the
church's doctrine and the legal or civil question.' For Weakland, this
situation required thoughtful conversation and listening to women. This
was an example of his theology and style of Benedictine leadership – a
vision of a church and world in dialogue.

The primary goal of the 'listening sessions' was to provide Weakland
with 'feedback', in order to develop a major pastoral statement on
abortion. This action rested on years of experience in parish and
diocesan-wide councils, consultations and synods. As the release date for
Weakland's abortion pastoral and final report of the 'listening sessions'
approached in May 1990, both local and national news organizations
wanted access to Weakland for interviews and copies of the text. There
was significant interest and pressure to report on Weakland since his was
a different style from that of Cardinal O'Connor.

Despite all the carefully worded statements, the 21 May headline in the
Milwaukee Sentinel read: 'Weakland: Pro-Choice Could be OK: Stance
at Odds with US Conference of Bishops'. Reaction to this article was
immediate. To some, Weakland had been perceived as 'breaking ranks
among the Catholic bishops on abortion'. Others looked unkindly on
Weakland's critical statements about the pro-life movement. Weakland
told me: 'My problems came mostly with the *Sentinel* headlines. People
don't read, they only read headlines. And those headlines influenced how
it was picked up by *USA Today*, and other papers.' He lamented: 'How
do you ever get anything under control after it's out there? That's one of
the major things with regard to the media . . . We as a church haven't

learned yet how to deal with all of that. I don't think we know how to do that effectively.'

I asked him about the role of the public media in presenting theological opinions. He replied: 'I am not a "yes" or "no" person . . . I hate that style. And especially in religion. I find I like to nuance everything and to me the subordinate clauses are as important as the declarative sentences and I like to leave doors open. So that's always hard for me because the press will cut out all my adjectives, all my clauses and leave me bare.' Then he shifted focus, and added: 'We are concentrating too much on news media, and television . . . I find other things happening. So for the first time now you are getting some of the major magazines . . . whether it be the *Atlantic* or the *New Yorker* carrying a totally different kind of analysis of church affairs. They are willing to get someone knowledgeable to do a full piece on an aspect which you cannot expect a newspaper writer to do. And I see more hope there.'

IV. Conclusion

In Weakland, O'Connor and Bernardin one sees an almost continual interplay of church and press, for better or worse, which defines their individual public, civic and religious roles as moral teachers and community leaders. This connection between church and press is not simply an extra feature extending their message and influence. Rather, it is the pervasive culture in which their messages and moral teachings are understood. This situation has heightened conflict among political and religious groups in the United States and has puzzled observers, including the press. What makes abortion even more complex is the extent to which it becomes a political issue and impacts on the lives and careers of churchmen and candidates for public office alike.

My study of these church leaders simply confirms the point made by the historian David O'Brien that the American Catholic church does not have a coherent understanding of its public role.[8] These forms of cultural Catholicism – organizational, intellectual and political – are reflected in the voices of Bernardin, O'Connor and Weakland and influence the tone, perception and presentation of abortion as a moral concern. I am not saying that Bernardin, O'Connor and Weakland disagree on the church's moral teaching about abortion; rather, their individual presentation or style of communication does affect how this teaching is understood.

Consequently, one senses the frustration among the American bishops that important positions on moral issues, and the news of religion generally, are poorly reported in the American media and, thus, not taken seriously by many people. Such insights, if accurate, underscore the tensions between the church and the press as one example of competing discourses inherent within post-modern society.

To my mind, the central challenge for church leadership today is how to create a persuasive and effective public presence, a presence that distinguishes between matters of public policy and religious belief. If there is a 'Catholic moment' today, it would be the church's public commitment to enter into the conversation about the moral crises of our times – one that brings to the discussion not an imposition of moral authority with threatened sanctions, but rather the sharing of the moral wisdom of its people, drawing from its wealth of organizational, political, intellectual and spiritual resources, a wisdom that could benefit Catholics as well as the nation.

Notes

1. David Shaw, 'Abortion in America' series, *Los Angeles Times*, 1–4 July 1990. Data cited in this series were taken from S. Robert Lichter el al., 'Roe v. Webster: Media Coverage of the Abortion Debate', *Media Monitor*, Center for Media and Public Affairs, Washington DC (Vol. III, no. 8), October 1989; Jason DeParle, 'Beyond the Legal Right', *Washington Monthly*, Vol. 21, no. 3, April 1989.

2. Cardinal Bernardin, Interview, 26 November 1990: all subsequent quotations in the text were part of this interview.

3. 'Press Conference with Cardinal Bernardin', NCCB/USCC Official Proceedings, Catholic Television Network of America, 7 November 1989.

4. Robert N. Bellah, 'Leadership Viewed from the Vantage Point of American Culture', *Origins*, Vol. 20, no. 14, 13 September 1990.

5. Cardinal O'Connor, Interview, 10 December 1990: all subsequent quotations in the text were part of this interview.

6. See Ari Goldman, 'O'Connor Won't Meet Reporters After Masses', *New York Times*, Friday, 7 September 1990.

7. Archbishop Weakland, Interview, 2 November 1990: all subsequent quotations in the text were part of this interview.

8. David O'Brien, *Public Catholicism*, New York 1989, 7.

Religion Observed: The Impact of the Medium on the Message

Kenneth L. Woodward

Since the editors of *Concilium* have asked me to be personal, I will focus on the journalistic world I know best: the national (indeed, international) news magazine. Although American in its origins, the news magazine is now a widely imitated form for packaging the week's news. It is also a bellwether, of sorts, by which we can measure the importance that the 'cultural elites' of the society or country attach to religion.

My more specific charge from *Concilium* is to comment on the advantages and disadvantages of writing about religion in a secular medium. But, as I will argue, the fact that a magazine is secular in outlook is less relevant than the possibilities and constraints inherent in the medium itself. My experience as a journalist confirms what various practitioners of the 'sociology of knowledge' have long argued: first, that institutions foster certain patterns of behaviour and perception;[1] second, that the practice of any craft creates a certain consciousness that goes a long way towards shaping, sometimes unconsciously, how the practitioner views the world. For example, there are journalists in television and in magazines whose minds are so disciplined by the tools of their trade that they can visualize how a story – even as it is developing – will look on the television screen or on the printed page.

The news magazine, then, is an institution which generates a certain 'craft consciousness'[2] which differentiates both its process and product from those of newspapers, television and other journalistic media. Thus, what I have to say about my experience as a journalist who covers the world of religion can be understood only within the context of the history and development of the news magazine as a distinct journalistic genre.

In my most sanguine moments, I like to think of the news magazine journalist as poor cousin to the cultural historian, as the latter has been described by the Dutch scholar Johan Huizinga. In his essay, 'The Task of Cultural History', Huizinga wrote that 'the forms of the past are the expressions of a spirit which [the cultural historian] attempts to understand, always viewing them in the thick of events'. Reporting on and in the midst of the 'thick of events', the journalist, in his own way, tries to discern the forms or patterns that best illuminate the meaning of those events. One major difference is that he does this against the pressure of a deadline.

What any journalist writes is dictated in large part by the pressures of time and space. The writer for the Associated Press, Reuters or another wire service has several deadlines a day and so is bound by the imperatives of that severe schedule. Context is not what we look for in a report off the wires. The daily newspaper observes a more flexible schedule. The heart of a daily is that day's 'hard' news, but comprehensive newspapers also include longer, more thoughtful interpretative pieces that may require days, weeks or even months to prepare.

The form of the news magazine

From its inception, however, the news magazine has claimed the right and obligation to interpret even as it reports, and to entertain as well as inform. The entertainment is provided in the way the story is told. But so, often enough, is the interpretation. Moreover, the length of most news magazine stories is quite short when compared to the amount of information that they typically try to convey. Conciseness, in short, is the distinguishing characteristic of a news magazine story. It is also the form's most demanding discipline as well as the writer's most exasperating constraint.

Henry Luce, the co-founder and first editor of *Time*, invented the modern news magazine in the 1920s. Initially, it is worth recalling, Luce hired bright young men out of prestige universities (mainly his own *alma mater*, Yale) merely to rewrite what the newspapers that week had reported. Only gradually did *Time* develop its own world-wide network of reporters, and only in the 1970s did it, following its rival, *Newsweek*, publish individual bylines so that the reader could identify the author(s). Thus, for four decades, *Time* spoke with a single, omniscient and often imperious voice. Reading a *Time* story, one would never suppose that it was the product of several human hands.

Time's impersonality, however, hid the fact that Luce had created a new division of journalistic labour. Those who reported on the week's events did not write the stories. And those who wrote the stories rarely spoke to, much less met, the people they wrote about. In turn, both reporters and writers found their copy copiously edited to achieve a striking uniformity of tone and outlook. '*Time* says' summoned up an image of omniscience that more traditional journalists, who both reported and wrote their own stories, often reviled as 'group journalism', but which other publishers just as often envied.

With its familiar red cover border, *Time* assumed a genuinely iconic presence within American culture. Inside, all of human experience was unvaryingly divided into departments whose generic, one-word headings – 'World', 'Nation', 'Science', 'Religion', 'Books' and the like – gave the impression that these categories had been dictated at the dawn of – what else? – time itself. Readers were made to feel that what they held in their hands contained all they needed to know about what had happened in the known journalistic world the previous week. Moreover, Luce's writers and editors did not hesitate to use elevated words and sonorous sentences: readers may have had to consult a dictionary from time to time, but this only enhanced the impression that they were participating in a higher, privileged realm of insight, erudition and discourse. From its very origins, then, the news magazine did not present an argument to be rebutted. Rather, it arranged its editorial material in such a way that the argument or ideology – and in most political and other matters *Time* was usually ideological – was contained in the narrative presentation itself. The reader either accepted the story as reality or did not. In this regard, Luce was a publishing genius, and for those who accepted its authority, *Time* was both mirror and lamp.

In its use of language, *Time* borrowed a number of techniques from literature – for example, focussing on idiosyncrasies of dress or speech to convey character – which have since been widely imitated by journalists working in other genres. Of these techniques, one continues to set the news magazine apart from other genres. Long before contemporary 'theologians of story' discovered the importance of the narrative line, Luce recognized – perhaps 'dictated' is more precise – that a news magazine story should have the internal consistency, economy, trajectory and resolution of a good short story. (Many of Luce's writers, it should be noted, were gifted stylists, such as the poet and distinguished translator of Homer, Robert Fitzgerald, the novelist James Agee and essayist Dwight McDonald.) Of course, the facts of a story, like the facts of life, are seldom so obliging. Indeed, the chief criticism of *Time* was that it never let a contrary fact get in the way of tellling a good story. Nonetheless, this is the basic form we have come to expect from news magazines, and it is the form with which, week after week, news magazine journalists must wrestle. *Time* was (and remains) a secular magazine, as was evident from its format. Stories pertaining to religion were sequestered in the department with that heading. This had the effect of confining religious reporting to the activities of religious institutions and their leaders. But Luce, the son of Presbyterian missionaries, was a religious man, and he took the subject seriously. Thus, he regularly featured religious issues, ideas and personalities on *Time*'s cover, including full-dress journalistic portraits of theologians like Reinhold Niebuhr, Paul Tillich and John Courtney Murray. Luce's editorial decision to 'puff' a new evangelist named Billy Graham is widely credited with launching Graham's career. In this respect, *Time* did, in its coverage of religion at least, mirror rather well the religious landscape of the 1940s, 1950s and early 1960s, although it is a nice hermeneutical question how much *Time* itself shaped perceptions and memories of that landscape.

It is not enough, therefore, to label a news magazine 'secular' just because it is not published under religious auspices. What matters, as I have suggested, are the operating assumptions about the significance of religion in human affairs. Like the intellectual class in general (and academics in particular), news magazine editors tend to regard religious ideas and identities as essentially peripheral to public life. They also tend to be unaware of the extraordinary variety of religion in the United States. Historically, America has been the birthplace of many new religions as well as home to many transplanted and transformed traditions from abroad. Indeed, the pluralism and fluidity of American religion, so bewildering to European journalists, only compounds the difficulty editors face in trying to decide how much attention they should give to religion.

My job, as one news magazine's resident 'expert' on religion, is to recognize when and how religion makes a difference in the way people think, feel and act – as individuals and as groups – and then try to convince my colleagues that these differences are worth reporting. The most important religion stories, therefore, are rarely about religion alone but almost always about something else as well: politics, economics, morality, psychology, social movements, education, scholarship, science, international affairs – the reach is as wide and diverse as human experience itself. As I see it, my field is the culture of religion, on the one hand, and the relationship between religion and the wider, secular 'overculture' on the other. Therefore, what matters to me is the value editors attach to religion as measured by two criteria: the amount of space it regularly devotes to religious subjects and institutions and the extent to which religious perspectives are included in the magazine's presentation of public issues, events and controversies.

Newsweek, as it happens, has never taken religion as seriously as Luce's *Time*. Before I joined *Newsweek* in 1964, the Religion section was handled by the education editor – a woman, which in those days was sure sign that the subject matter was held in low esteem. But news of international consequence was being made at Vatican Council II, and *Newsweek*'s editors were pleased to hire a Roman Catholic as Religion editor. During my job interview, *Newsweek*'s editor-in-chief, an indifferent Episcopalian, put only one – professionally astute – question to me. Could I, he wanted to know, be fair to the Council's conservatives? He recognized, of course, what many readers still do not: namely that controversy is the essence of what journalists consider news. Both progressives and conservatives in Rome came to see this, which is why both sides did what they could to shape the media's presentation of the drama that was Vatican II. Unfortunately, the converse of this axiom is that the 'Good News' – including the good that people do – seldom makes news. It is not surprising, therefore, that conservative institutions like the Vatican are inherently wary of the press.

Advantages and disadvantages

Writing about religion for a general-interest magazine has a number of advantages and disadvantages. The chief advantage is that a news magazine addresses a wider and more diverse audience than any religious magazine can hope to attract. The mass news media, as I choose to think of them, are what we have because we no longer have public squares, town meetings or even cafés. Because of the mass media, we are a public, and anyone who wishes to address that public must be prepared to accept certain linguistic and other trade-offs. Theologians and philosophers no less than physicians and scientists understand that they must sacrifice nuance as well as professional jargon if they want to communicate with the wider audience that mass media provide. Similarly, journalists who specialize (as most now do) within the mass media must master the art of translating the argot and complexities of experts into acceptable public discourse. Indeed, finding the appropriate words, images and analogies to mediate complicated ideas to the lay reader is the primary and routine challenge such a journalist faces.

In this regard, I recall a humorous but telling early experience. One of the first articles I wrote for *Newsweek* identified the moral and other theologians who had been appointed by Pope Paul VI as a commission to advise him on the issue of contraception. It was, I thought, a straightforward piece of reporting. But in the editing process, *Newsweek*'s editor-in-chief objected to the term 'moral' theologian and directed that the defining adjective be deleted. Gradually, his reason became clear to me: Since some of the theologians were not identified as moral theologians, the editor thought readers would conclude – as he had – that anyone not so identified was, in fact, an *immoral* theologian. It is not a news magazine's province, he wanted me to know, to decide which theologians are moral and which are not.

A more typical and substantive example is illustrated by a cover story I wrote in 1970. On the Fourth of July that year, the evangelist Billy Graham presided at an 'Honour America' Day at the Washington Monument, an event that provided a news peg for a profile on Graham, who had risen to new heights of influence during the first administration of his friend, President Richard M. Nixon. To interpret Graham's meaning to American culture at that moment in his career, I made considerable use of the sociologist Robert Bellah's then-recent essay on 'the civil religion', using a quotation from Rousseau's *The Social Contract* to preface the story. The interpretative theme was that the sort of generalized and patriotic Christianity Graham preached had become America's civil religion under Nixon. A sub-theme was that Graham himself was given to political images in his own conception of Christianity; thus, the article closed with Graham's musing on the 'rewards' he expected in heaven: 'And each of them must be tremendous crowns – or maybe planets to rule.'

Another, often overlooked, advantage of the secular media is that a writer in charge of a section like Religion is serviced by a network of bureaus whose correspondents he can call upon for reporting. For instance, *Newsweek*'s cover story last year on personal prayer, 'Talking to God', utilized files from correspondence in diverse regions of the United States who interviewed a variety of individuals about their prayer habits. Similarly, for a 1992 story on Opus Dei, I utilized files from correspondents in Rome and Paris. Conversely, bureau correspondents regularly suggest stories, including those on religion, to the editors in New York. In this way editors can monitor trends both nationally and internationally.

A third resource news magazines frequently use is the public opinion poll. As it happens, *Newsweek* was the first organization (including religious organizations) to commission a poll of American Catholics on their attitudes towards their church. That occurred in 1967, just after the Council, and the results were woven into a cover story I wrote entitled: 'How US Catholics View Their Church'.

A fourth advantage is that, as *Newsweek*'s Religion editor, I automatically possess the credentials personally to interview virtually anyone I choose. In addition, *Newsweek* provides me with subscriptions to nearly twenty publications (many of them scholarly; some of them, like denominational newspapers, more expressive of the grass roots) which enable me to keep abreast of what is being thought and said. In short, a news magazine allows – and expects – me to be on top of what is happening in the world of religion. As a result, I am always learning. This also applies to other specialists on the magazine. The point is that in any given week, *Newsweek* collectively takes in far more information than it publishes.

Like other journalists, it should be noted, those who write for news magazines are heavily dependent upon the opinion of experts. Experts recognize this, which is why most are willing to put up with enquiring journalists. But the process can be abused. A writer can, if he or she chooses, quote only those experts with which he or she already agrees. Similarly, experts (especially theologians) have learned that they can shape public opinion through the mass media by defining how events ought to be understood. A classic case in point occurred in 1979 when the Catholic bishops of Latin America met in Puebla, Mexico. The press was barred from attending their deliberations; so were most of the progressive theologians who clustered around the event. But as the bishops' documents were issued, they were immediately interpreted for the press at briefings by those self-same theologians. As a result, what the bishops said passed through a progressivist prism of interpretation before the news reached the public.

The disadvantages of reporting on religion in a news magazine are just as real but not so easily explained. First, most readers do not realize that journalists – at newspapers, but especially at new magazines – must compete with each other for space. It's a zero-sum game, since there is a limited number of columns each week for editorial material. And that space, in turn, is affected to some degree by the amount of advertising pages sold, since the advertising pages carry the editorial pages. The arbiters of this internal editorial market place are the editors whose news judgment determines which stories get printed. The system works like this. As Religion editor, I suggest one or more stories to a senior editor who is responsible for several other specialty sections. He then decides which among the stories are the strongest candidates for that week's issue. He – or she – then presents a list to a story conference of all senior editors and managing editors. Barring a late-breaking news event, these then are the stories that appear in that week's issue. This is, of course, also how television, radio and newspapers operate.

Given the competitive nature of this internal market it should be obvious that there is no short or even coherent answer to the question: how do you decide which events to cover or which stories to write? Writers are at the mercy of their editors and the editors are often at odds with each other. My point is that the system of story selection is far more arbitrary than professional journalists generally like to admit. It doesn't take much news judgment to decide what is important in national and world affairs: some events *must* be covered, and the only question is how much space to give each story. But news magazine editors also regard each issue as a package, and in deciding which among competing stories to print they strive for a mix of articles that will appeal to a diverse audience. Increasingly, moreover, the quality of pictures available for illustrating articles also determines (as it does in television) which stories get published and at what length.

Of all the decisions editors make, the choice of which story should be featured on the cover is the most important. One reason is economic: although news stand sales account for only about ten per cent of issues sold each, those sales – rather than circulation – provide the primary yardstick by which professionals who place advertising measure the comparative vitality of competing magazines. A news magazine deemed editorially 'hot' draws the advertising dollar even though it may have a smaller circulation. The other reason is editorial: like the choice of what to put on the front page of a newspaper, each cover story is a statement about the magazine's ability to discern what is most relevant, new or important. It is, in short, a declaration of that magazine's editorial perspicuity.

The choice of stories

Obviously, the degree of frustration writers experience is directly related to how often their stories are accepted or rejected. Hence the second disadvantage of writing about religion in a secular publication is related to the first: one is wholly dependent upon the judgment of editors who may or may not have any interest in religion. In this regard there has been a distinct downward trend in the number of stories appearing in both *Newsweek* and *Time*. In the 1960s and 1970s, I was expected to be prepared to write one story of at least a page in length and two shorter stories. In those days, the Religion section appeared, as an average, in three out of every four issues. Twice a year we also produced cover stories in religion. Today, however, the Religion section appears little more than twice a month, and some years there are no covers devoted to religion.

There are several reasons for this trend. First, in order to deal effectively with shifts in society and culture, news magazines have, of necessity, become more flexible. With the addition of new sections devoted to the family and to aging, to name only two, there are now many more departments than there is editorial space to accommodate them all each week. (Time has virtually abandoned the convention of regular weekly news departments, including Religion.) Secondly, the audience for news magazines has changed, and with it publishing's economic environment. The immediacy and pervasiveness of television has forced news magazines to shorten stories to match their readers' reduced attention-spans, and dramatically to increase the amount of space devoted to pictorial display. Today, the layout of news magazines more resembles the old *Life*, which was essentially a picture magazine, than the old *Time*. Moreover, I would argue, the generations of magazine readers now in their twenties, thirties and even forties are profoundly a-literate: that is, they *can* read but would rather watch. In matters of religion, they are more eclectic and less rooted in definable traditions; this alone limits the level of familiarity with religious concepts that I can assume in my readers.

For example, when Martin Luther King Jr led his famous civil rights march into Selma, Alabama in 1965, he was joined by thousands of clergy and religious leaders in a massive public demonstration of interfaith and interracial solidarity. I tried to capture this in the opening sentence of my story: 'Like the lame to Lourdes they came – priests, nuns, ministers and rabbis, several thousands of all – sensing somehow that God was stirring the waters in Selma, Alabama.' Today, I doubt that I could use the Lourdes analogy because so few of our readers would recognize it.

But I suspect that there is a fourth and far more significant reason why religion is not covered like it used to be. We know from numerous studies that those who work in the national media are much less religious than American society as a whole. We also know that most Americans are religious but that these religious convictions are vastly under-represented in the journalistic class. Put another way, we know that the people who create network television news, our national newspapers such as the *New York Times* and the news magazines, constitute a professional elite or sub-culture which is far more secular than the culture of their viewers and readers. Like an eye with a detached retina, they do not see – and in many cases do not want to acknowledge – the saliency of religion in American life. Moreover, I also believe – and here I am not alone – that the editors of the national media tend to edit for each other – that is to say, for editors of other magazines who, like themselves, are not only ignorant of but often fearful and dismissive of religion. Even in New York, the circle of magazine editors is quite small; at least seven national magazines are now edited by people who formally worked at *Newsweek*. What we are witnessing, I suppose, is journalistic validation of the sociologist C. Wright Mills' theory of the 'circulation of elites'.

If we look at what *does* get published about religion, certain patterns become obvious. First, American news magazines – like the mass media in general – pay far more attention to Roman Catholics than to any other denomination in American society. The Catholics' only competition for attention comes from the emerging evangelical-fundamentalist movement which in the last decade has made its presence felt in politics. Attention, of course, is not admiration, and in the case of the fundamentalists their image as the backbone of the political 'Religious Right' has made them journalism's favourite whipping boy.

Conversely, the least noticed religious groups are those liberal Protestant denominations which, in Luce's era, still constituted the nation's religious establishment. In this respect, I would argue that the lack of media attention paid to the activities and pronouncements of these 'old-line' denominations is a fairly accurate reflection of how little these traditions elicit interest and support from their own declining memberships. In short, it is not simply that Roman Catholics and evangelical Protestants constitute the two largest religious 'families' in the United States. Nor is it simply that these two groups are perceived to be politically powerful. (In fact, however, we know that Catholics do not vote as a bloc, at least in national elections.) Rather, they attract media notice because each in its own way also manifests distinctive and discernible beliefs, convictions and patterns of behaviour: they stand for something. Put another way, in order to be considered politically and socially significant, a religious group must first be identifiable – to its own members and to the public. And identity is something which the liberal denominations no longer possess.

Opportunities for the future

Regarding the future of the news magazine as a journalistic institution, there are several outside pressures which are transforming the genre. The first is economic. Over the last five years, all international news-gathering organizations, print as well as television, based in the United States have been forced to cut back staff, especially in the number of reporters in the field. Many newspapers no longer have a religion writer or regular religion section. Most American television networks have closed their bureaus in Rome and other European capitals. As a result, the capacity to report in depth has been seriously diminished.

The second pressure is cultural: today, no news magazine commands anything like the institutional authority of Luce's *Time*. Nor, in the United States, does any one news programme on television. (In this regard, I suspect Europe and Asia are different.) Just as the proliferation of cable channels has reduced the impact of network, so the proliferation of special-interest magazines, narrowly focused newsletters and the like have weakened the cultural impact of magazines aimed at 'the general interest'. Indeed, I would argue that my earlier identification of the mass media with the creation of a 'public' is fast becoming history. As the magazine of 'general interest' is replaced by a smorgasbord of publications targeted at specific interests and enthusiasms, the 'public' appears to be dissolving into a series of discrete sub-cultures, much like universities. The impact of this trend on the coverage religion in news magazines is already evident: increasingly, news magazine stories about religion focus only on issues, events and trends which have broad cultural rather than narrow (e.g. denominational) impact.

Third, American society has become so media conscious – mainly because of the omnipresence of television – that the lines between genuine news gathering and reporting on the one hand, and entertainment, advertising and public relations on the other have been blurred. Americans now speak routinely of 'media events', conscious of the fact that certain events would not take place if journalists (again, especially television) were not there to record them. In short, we are witnessing an increase in pseudo-events.

One major effect of these changes on news magazines has been to give writers greater licence to voice their own opinions – 'attitude' it is called – in much the same way that Luce's *Time* routinely passed judgment on the events it reported. The difference is that writers now do this in their own voice and under their own name. Thus, the old authority of the magazine is now exercised by individual writers whose attitude tends to mark the difference between news magazines. In short, journalists themselves have become media celebrities and, seduced by television, are pressured to pronounce – to perform – more often than to report. As a result, the public tends to learn from journalists more about what they think than about what others think. Since the culture of journalism is generally ignorant of and often hostile to religion, the effect of all this is further to sequester religious conversation, even about public events, in the private sphere of specialty religious publications and television programmes.

But much as I regret these changes, I also can discern some opportunities. So many transformations are occurring in the nation's fundamental institutions and attitudes – towards the family, gender-relations, the maintenance of communities and the work place – that issues of fundamental concern require constant airing and debate. And to the degree that religion speaks to and embodies basic attitudes about human existence, these changes offer renewed opportunities for bringing religious perspectives and critiques to bear on issues that affect society as a whole. Indeed, many new social movements – feminism and the gay-rights movement are two of the most obvious – function for many of their adherents as the equivalent of religion. All this is, or should be, grist for journalists of religion.

Notes

1. On institutions as patterns of behaviour, see Robert N. Bellah, Richard Madsen, William M. Sullivan, Ann Swidler and Steven M. Tipton, *The Good Society*, New York 1991.
2. On the idea of craft consciousness, see Joseph Bensman and Robert Lilienfeld, *Craft and Consciousness: Occupational Technique and the Development of World Images*, New York 1973.

'Young Man, Come Down from the Pulpit!' The Experiences of a Theologian in Secular Political Journalism

Arnd Henze

I have been asked to reflect, in a case study, on how Christian values can be 'incorporated' into a secular medium. I should say straight away that this question seems to me to be too static, to be too much like a one-way street: as if it were simply a matter of 'applying' fixed ethical criteria in a straight line. What I am in fact interested in is the interplay between faith and life, and I see the secular as a challenge. For journalism has to do with the 'secular' world in its brokenness and contradictoriness, and faith often sees it as 'God's good creation' only contrary to all appearances. Because I want to reflect on personal experience here, first I shall hang my remarks on a few events in my life; then I shall relate my understanding of journalistic work to the three central themes of social ethics: 'justice, peace and the preservation of creation'.

My first attempts at journalism go back to my schooldays. I began in a local newspaper, and then at the age of seventeen worked on a popular radio programme for young people. It was a phase of trying things out, and not just dealing with topics and forms. Working as an eighteen-year-old for a programme with a public which ran into millions confronted me at an early stage with a particular danger of the profession: vanity. I still regard coping productively with one's public role as one of the greatest challenges for journalists (a problem which is also faced to a limited degree by pastors). Whereas what came first of all was delight at being a reporter and a presenter, the work really took shape when I did my alternative to military service as a conscientious objector in an advisory centre for those on drugs. Confrontation with young addicts, with the homeless and the unemployed, with the desperate conditions in prisons and psychiatric hospitals – all this changed my perception of reality, which had been shaped by my middle-class upbringing, and thus also my journalistic concerns. It is no coincidence that my decision to study theology took shape at the very time when my reporting became more committed and partisan. At that time I had not heard of the 'preferential option for the poor', but the partisan standpoint expressed in that phrase shaped both my journalist work and my interest in becoming a pastor.

After my compulsory service, my main work for just on two years was for the peace movement in Germany. This included the preparation of major demonstrations and campaigns against the stationing of new nuclear missiles in Europe. At this time we had daily experience of the ambivalence of the media: on the one hand we had to give a comprehensive account of our arguments and actions, because public discussion is necessarily shaped by the media. On the other, every day we were shocked by the caricatures and falsifications of this discussion by the media. Instead of presenting facts and arguments, before major demonstrations the media almost exclusively speculated on possible clashes – and when everything remained peaceful, the event was regularly trivialized as an unpolitical folk festival. From this, many of my friends in social movements concluded sweepingly that they should dismiss the media as 'hostile', as critical of authority and corrupt. By contrast, I am still convinced that the caricature of reality is not an essential characteristic of journalism, but its perversion. Today I know from my own experience that the boundary between serious and perverted journalism does not lie simply between different media and colleagues, but has to be redrawn and responded to in daily decisions (in theological terms, this is the daily experience of guilt, which can have particularly devastating consequences in our profession).

During my study I wavered for a long time between the pastorate and journalism as a future career. That in the end I chose the former was in part a matter of chance, but behind the choice lay one reason in particular which at first sight may seem surprising: I was and am convinced that conditions in the 'secular' working world are freer, more honest and more humane than those in the churches. The two great churches in Germany are the second largest employer after the state. But instead of giving an example in their internal structures of shared responsibility, a capacity for reform and an ability to overcome conflicts, these institutions call for a loyalty which is based exclusively on hierarchy and bureaucracy. The freedom of the children of God comes up against its limits in church employment law. That is manifest in the Catholic church; the procedure is more subtle in the Protestant church, but no less effective. For want of a Christian culture which can tolerate disputes, the church's need for harmony becomes a disciplinary scourge which leaves little room for those with minds of their own or whose commitment is unconventional.

As the hierarchy automatically understands conflicts as a question of power, its disciplinary authority also ends with those who hold office. Therefore I still enjoy the freedom of belonging to the church as an honorary collaborator.

In contrast to the world of church work, any 'secular' place of work has the advantage that conflicts in it are not obscured by a pious ideology of harmony. There is at least the demand that the right to work and the distribution of spheres of competence should be based on the insight that different interests have to be balanced out. I do not expect from my employer more than reasonably fair rules to work by, which guarantee space for independent journalistic work. And my superiors do not expect me to love Westdeutscher Rundfunk, but they do expect me to show some commitment in my job. This secular matter-of-factness leaves incomparably more space, and in practice proves far more humane, than the demands of the church hierarchy for loyalty, which are so stamped with patriarchalism.

That also applies to the difference between public broadcasting and the church media. Of course our programmes are subject to massive pressure from political parties and lobbyists – and all too often people yield to this pressure. But the basic right of freedom of the press provides the intrinsic criterion for resisting political influence and attempts at censorship – and wherever editors have the courage to resist the lobbyists, they have all the arguments on their side. Church journalists do not have this weapon. As long as the independence of journalistic work is not recognized even in theory, the individual journalist is left at the mercy of the demands of hierarchy and bureaucracy for loyalty.

After my theological examination I had an intensive training in journalism, and for a year have been working as a television editor in foreign programmes at Westdeutscher Rundfunk. I live in a rented room in a clergy house, belong to the presbytery of my community, and occasionally preach at worship. Outwardly everything had turned out as well as could be. But that does not say much about the relationship between my professional life and the sphere of life of which I am an honorary member.

A rigorous separation of the two along the lines of a wrong understanding of the doctrine of two realms is quite out of the question for two reasons: it does not fit in with my own personal history, nor is it theologically tenable. Despite my affirmation of the secular structure of my work, I cannot exist in it fundamentally differently from the way in which I spend Sundays in church. But the opposite attempt, simply to understand journalism as a continuation of church work with other means, seems to me to be just as senseless. I remember a course on commentaries at the beginning of my journalistic training. The teacher (who also happened to be a theologian) came straight to the point. 'Young man, come down from the pulpit!' That remark stuck.

Neither separation nor confusion create a meaningful relationship between one's own value system and professional practice. The ethics of journalism develop out of daily discussion with colleagues who from different religious, philosophical and political traditions seek criteria for dealing responsibly with the possibilities and dangers of the medium. That this discussion still takes place at least in parts of public television is for me the decisive advantage of such television, and is the way in which it differs from commercial stations. I have never had to keep quiet about my church background among my colleagues. The church tradition of intolerance, dogmatism and inquisition prompts modesty rather than arrogance.

Conditions of journalism almost always follow the principle of 'trial and error'. There are just as many unsuccessful programmes as successful broadcasts. Above all, the increasing pressure of everyday events makes us all too often *react*, when with better preparation we should have provided our own emphases. New technological possibilities and a competition with commercial stations which has got out of control have made speed and live presence an idol. Live research on the programme rather than information which has been thoroughly checked is increasingly becoming the characteristic of the media. Television nowhere failed more dismally in recent years than in its coverage of the Gulf War. Programmes became the almost mindless instrument of propaganda, not out of conviction, but because of unprofessional preparation. There was no background knowledge about the Middle East, no knowledge of Islam (which was continually caricatured), no professional knowledge of the politics of security to provide the means of making a critical analysis of the pseudo-information of the military. Criticism rapidly became generalized moral indignation – which is useless against the propagandistic undertow of the affirmative which ultimately fewer and fewer colleagues were able to escape. The subsequent horror at the failure was considerable; it remains to be seen whether we have learned from it.

Except in special crises like the Gulf War or the 1991 Moscow Putsch, the foreign affairs department in which I work is primarily responsible for providing detailed background and only partially for presenting topical news reports. That gives us more room for manoeuvre, both in finding topics and in shaping our approach. I see our magazine programmes and reports as a supplement, if not a corrective, to the one-sidedness of topical new programmes. The focal points of our programme seem to me to be very close to the themes of ecumenical church discussion: 'justice, peace and the preservation of creation'.

1. Justice

In the dispute within the church there is a confrontation between the hierarchical tradition of piety and authority and the 'preferential option for the poor'. In journalism there are comparable fronts: 'court' reporting on the one hand and critical reporting on the other. Just as liberation theology appeals to the biblical and earliest Christian tradition, so the insistence on the separation of journalism from power appeals to a fundamental democratic principle: the constitutional concern has always been to guarantee freedom of the press in a dimension which is critical of domination. The 'preferential option for the poor' takes on weight for journalistic ethics above all when poverty is understood not only in economic terms but also, as Gustavo Gutiérrez understands it, as marginalization. I think that our reporting is best where it measures the political action of the powerful by the effects of their policy on those concerned. It is not generalized pictures on poverty but reports narrated with sensitivity which restore dignity to the victims of injustice and oppression and give them a voice in the public sphere. Marginalization is overcome not with the journalist who knows better but when people themselves with their own inalienable history have a say – in all their brokenness and contradictoriness. Fortunately, in our study of theology Gustavo Gutiérrez impressed on us that the 'preferential option for the poor' does not hold because the poor are better people, but because they are poor. Social kitsch is no use to anyone.

However, one dilemma is insoluble: the proximity which good and impressive reporting must achieve is at the same time an invasion of people's privacy, in two respects. First, working with a camera team to a large degree necessarily has quite secular technical consequences. Whether we want to or not, we disturb a house or a neighbourhood. Secondly, in showing a film we make public private experiences of the protagonists. We cannot foresee all the consequences that this will have for those concerned.

This dilemma is insoluble. Any reporter can keep exercising his or her conscience or discussing with colleagues where the line is to be drawn between necessary proximity and cynical voyeurism, when the camera must be switched off or a shot must not be broadcast – and the danger of error can never be excluded. Nevertheless, that there is still awareness of this conflict in public television marks the fundamental difference between us and commercial stations, for whom any means is legitimate for securing high ratings.

2. Peace

Like many of my colleagues, I am a conscientious objector. I accept the ecumenical confession that 'War is against God's will'. Reports from war zones play a large part in our broadcasts. I know only a few colleagues who have open sympathy for military stances or even for armed force. That one gets used to it is a greater problem. Since the end of the Cold War, conflicts old and new have flared up all over the place. Violence has returned to Europe again in a cruel way with the war in former Yugoslavia. As journalists we cannot suppress the reality of wars. The ethical and professional challenge, though, is to prevent people getting used to the omnipresence of violence. I think that this is possible at various levels.

There are news pictures the information value and expressive images of which are virtually nil. Nevertheless, we keep seeing them every evening: random detached shots of exploding grenades, burning houses, charred corpses, screaming women. No viewer would notice if a report from the Caucasus were read out over such pictures from Sarajevo. They prevent any understanding of the specific background and causes of any war. I believe that a choice to limit the quantity of such pictures in war reports is urgently necessary for the sake of both relevant information and its emotional effect.

Pictures of the liberation of the Auschwitz death camp terrified me and many others when we were young. That was almost twenty years ago. Pictures of massacres and other atrocities nowadays just bounce off the young – and not only them.

Pictures of weeping members of families have also lost their expressiveness for viewers. So the task of conveying the sorrow and suffering in a way that goes beyond stereotyped metaphors and evokes compassion among viewers faces a completely new challenge. To give just one example of what form this might take: in Sarajevo there is a cellist who for a year played every day at a place in the city where people had been killed shortly beforehand. Each day a different place, each day a different sacrifice, but always the same quiet song of mourning, Albinoni's Adagio. A quiet portrait of this cellist, narrated without sentiment, would communicate more of the inhumanity of this war than all the reports of terror put together.

Anyone who switches on the television necessarily gets the impression that war and violence are normality, and peace is the exception. We must deliberately work against this trend in our programme planning. To depict the earth as a hopeless vale of tears not only produces a caricature of reality, but also deceives the viewer over the vital hope that peace is a real possibility in the world. This is all the more the case with reports from the so-called Third World, which is depicted publicly almost always only in connection with war, hunger and chaos. With their one-sided choice of themes, the media strengthen anxieties which are there anyway and the desire of 'fortress Europe' to shut itself off from the misery in the world. Our programme planning must show at least as much interest in the peaceful rebuilding of Eritrea as in the civil war in Somalia or in southern Sudan.

3. The preservation of creation

Ecumenical discussion has brought out the connection between global environment problems and the injustice in the world economy. This connection has been brought out in many public television programmes – not only in connection with the Environment Summit in Rio. The media have an opportunity to bring geographically far-flung places tangibly near. Without the media, the catastrophe over the Tchernobyl nuclear reactor would still have been universally hushed up – for the accident puts the use of nuclear power all over the world in question. Without the media, chemical businesses would have found it easier to produce products detrimental to the environment in the so-called Third World. Without the media, the destruction of the rain forest would still seem a regional problem for South America or Asia. The media have made a decisive contribution in describing these devastating problems.

Reporting on the environment must not be trivialized – but we must not talk in the downfall of the world either. We must find journalistic forms which can counter the all-embracing fatalism and arouse hope. I am not thinking of the idiotic optimism of the commercial stations, who counter horror stories about misery and poverty with the healthy world of the soap operas. We must discover and tell stories which show that it is worthwhile and even enjoyable to join in the real world with its problems and threats. It is no coincidence that it is such positive examples which provoke the greatest reactions from viewers. After a recent broadcast on energy saving there were thousands of requests for practical tips. Many pastors know the difficulty when preaching: they are meant to preach the gospel, but all that they can think of is images for describing an oppressive reality. And in order to find a more optimistic line, they take refuge in abstract phrases of dogmatic christology, offer stones instead of bread.

Here pastors and journalists are in the same boat: both must sharpen their gaze for the many thousand stories of hope that can be found all over the world.

Translated by John Bowden

Veritatis Splendor

Lisa Sowle Cahill

The new encyclical takes its lead from the problem of objectivity and relativism in ethics, which is critically important in contemporary ethics for many reasons. In Europe and North America, postmodern philosophy has thrown into doubt both Enlightenment reason's efforts to reach universal truths, and the introspective, self-transcending identity of the 'self' or 'subject'. All claims about human nature and timeless human values are now suspect. The critical, postmodern suspicion of 'truth' coalesces with Western political traditions, especially prevalent in North America, which centre on freedom, autonomy, and privacy. In the political arena, modern Western cultures tend to resolve moral uncertainty procedurally, not substantively. In the face of general lack of agreement on the common good, and despair of ever achieving consensus, they settle for freedom and informed choice in moral decisions. Examples abound in bioethics policy debates about euthanasia, infertility therapies, and abortion.

When we broaden the question of moral relativism to the international situation, we meet multiple competing claims to cultural, religious, and ethnic supremacy, accompanied by longlasting and bitter violence. Both the hopelessness of some situations, as in Eastern Europe, and tentative resolutions such as the Arab-Israeli peace initiative, warn of the importance of non-relative ideals of human dignity and rights.

Moreover, Christianity lives in an intercultural setting. Roman Catholicism itself incorporates many cultural traditions, and must in local cultures also take up dialogue with other religions and moral outlooks. And the emergence of the many 'theologies of liberation' around the globe demonstrates both that calls for political and cultural change must be appropriate to their situations, and that their effectiveness relies in the end on a sense of common humanity.

Against an overly relativistic respect for pluralism, *Veritatis Splendor* appeals to the natural law tradition, with its confidence in reasonable discernment of the values that people of different cultures and eras hold in common. The encyclical affirms that 'the natural law expresses the dignity of the human person and lays the foundation for his fundamental rights and duties, it is universal in its precepts and its authority extends to all mankind. *This universality does not ignore the individuality of human beings*, nor is it opposed to the absolute uniqueness of each person.' Nonetheless, it aims at a 'communion of persons' (51). The conviction that, despite cultural differences, morality at its most essential level is based on our common humanity, is at the heart of the modern papal social encyclicals, and grounds the legitimacy of the Church's voice on social and policy issues today. The lasting contribution of *Veritatis Splendor* may be its affirmation of objectivity in moral thinking, encouraging a renewal the Thomist tradition of natural law against postmodern relativism, and the absolutization of free choice as a moral value.

This contribution is more than likely to be undermined, however, by a second agenda of the encyclical, which is to restrain the kind of theological debate which advances scholarly inquiry in most Western institutions of higher education. The encyclical seems to have been composed less around a constructive, encouraging, and potentially cross-cultural message, than around condemning errors. It attacks exaggerated versions of 'autonomous ethics', 'fundamental option', and 'proportionalism'; reasserts the centrality in Catholic ethics of 'instrinsically evil acts', mortal sin, and church authority; and warns bishops to be vigilant toward pure doctrine and to protect the faithful from any danger of error (110, 169). Theological faculties are presumed to have a mandate from the local ordinary (110); moral theologians must not only refrain from public displays of disagreement, but must not even entertain any 'internal' questioning of teaching (165); and bishops should take away the name 'Catholic' from institutions that fail to abide by doctrinal requirements (116).

This agenda subverts the first message of the encyclical in at least two ways. First, members of the press, of the moral theological community, and of the episcopacy are likely to focus on the immediate juridical implications of the encyclical. Of course, this tendency will be reinforced if some members of the hierarchy use it as part of a net of documents woven to catch 'dissenters'. Second, and more theologically troublesome, the encyclical asserts that '[o]nly Christian faith' points the way to a true understanding of human nature (112), and that Catholic doctrine holds all the answers, no matter what 'the limitations of the human arguments employed' (165). Hence, it veers toward a fideism inconsistent with Catholic moral tradition and ultimately destructive of its best insights. While the first sections of the encyclical defend the universality of the natural law, the concluding sections define the moral life primarily as a 'confession' of an a 'witness' to faith (89), and commends revelation over reason as the source of moral knowledge.

Some interpreters, whether in hope or fear, may locate the importance of this encyclical in its association of contraception with intrinsic evil (123). Catholics would be much more effective spokespersons for objective sexual morality in every culture if we could focus our energies instead on the bigger issues about which we fundamentally agree, such as the positive, interrelated values of mutual respect, commitment, and parenthood. It will be a shame to the drafters and implementers of this encyclical if it results only further accusations and divisions in the Church.

Finally, the language of *Veritatis Splendor* is unrelentingly and gratuitously sexist. This failure is especially appalling in a document which aims to address the norms of sexual behaviour which so affect women's status. Official teaching is again singularly unresponsive to women's sensibilities in defining the 'human' good. A concluding section on Mary, no doubt intended to be pastoral, portrays her in stereotypically feminine terms as a compassionate and merciful mother to 'man'. 'She understands sinful man and loves him with a Mother's love' (121). This sort of plety only supports those who claim that the church's interpretations of sexual 'nature' are nothing but cultural products, and patriarchal ones at that.

Lisa Sowle Cahill

The editors of the Special Column are Norbert Greinacher and Bas van Iersel. The content of the Special Column does not necessarily reflect the views of the Editorial Board of Concilium.

Contributors

JOHN A. COLEMAN SJ was born in San Francisco in 1937. He holds advanced degrees in sociology from the University of California, Berkeley, and did advanced study in theology at the University of Chicago. He is the author or editor of over ten books, including *An American Strategic Theology*. He serves as the editor-in-chief for the Isaac Haecker series in American culture and religion and is currently Professor of Religion and Society at the Graduate Theological Union in Berkeley, California.
Address: The Jesuit School of Theology at Berkeley, 1735 LeRoy Avenue, Berkeley, CA 94709, USA.

JOHN M. STAUDENMAIER SJ is Professor of History at the University of Detroit Mercy, where he teaches the history of United States technology, engineering ethics and related seminars. His *Technology's Storytellers: Reweaving the Human Fabric*, Cambridge, Mass. 1985, received the Alpha Sigma Nu award for 1986; the book studies the first two decades of historiographic development of the Society for the History of Technology (founded 1958). Currently he is working on a study of Henry Ford as a cultural symbol of twentieth-century Modernist beliefs in America. He regularly lectures to secular and Catholic audiences on the relationship between technological design and cultural values.
Address: Dept. of History: History of Technology, University of Detroit Mercy, 4001 W McNichols Rd, P.O. Box 19900, Detroit, MI 48219–0900 USA.

JOAN HEMELS was born in 1944; he studied history and publicity at the Catholic University of Nijmegen and journalism at the Catholic Institute for Journalism. After working in the University of Nijmegen for many years, and teaching the history of the press, propaganda and public opinion at the University of Amsterdam, in 1987 he was appointed Professor of Communications there; in addition he has been visiting professor in the universities of Salzburg, Bochum, Eichstätt, Louvain and Mainz, and in 1993 he was also appointed *extraordinarius* Professor at the Catholic

University of Louvain. His most recent book, *De Pers onder het juk van een fiscale druk*, Amsterdam 1992, contains a bibliography of his publications.
Address: Kronsingel 23, NL-6581 BK Malden, The Netherlands.

WILLIAM E. BIERNATZKI, a Jesuit brother, was born in Niles, Michigan, USA, in 1931. He studied at Saint Louis University. Since 1989, he has been research director of the Centre for the Study of Communication and Culture, in London. Previously, he was Professor of Anthropology at Sogang University, Seoul, Korea. He has done anthropological and sociological field research in Korea, the Philippines and Vietnam. His publications include *Roots of Acceptance: The Intercultural Communication of Religious Meanings*, Rome 1991, and (co-authored) *Korean Catholicism in the '70s: A Christian Community Comes of Age*, Maryknoll, NY 1975. He is editor of the quarterly, *Communication Research Trends*.
Address: Centre for the Study of Communication and Culture, 221 Goldhurst Terrace, London NW6 3EP, England.

MIKLÓS TOMKA was born in 1941; he studied economics and sociology in Budapest, Leuven and Leiden, and taught in Budapest, where he is now Professor of the Sociology of Religion. He has also been a visiting professor in Bamberg and Innsbruck. A co-founder of the Hungarian Pastoral Institute (in 1989), he is also Director of the Hungarian Catholic Social Academy and head of the Hungarian Religious Research Centre (both also from the same year).
Address: H–1171 Budapest, Váviz u.4, Hungary.

JOHANN BAPTIST METZ was born in Auerbach, Bavaria, in 1928 and ordained priest in 1954. He has doctorates in both philosophy and theology and is currently Professor of Fundamental Theology in the University of Münster. Of his many publications, *Theology of the World* (1969) and *Faith in History and Society* are available in English; his most recent books are *Lateinamerika und Europa: Dialog der Theologien* (1988); *Welches Christentum hat Zukunft?* (1990); *Gottespassion* (1991); and *Augen für die Anderen* (1991).
Address: Kapitelstrasse 14, D 4400 Münster, Germany.

GREGORY BAUM was born in Berlin in 1923; since 1940 he has lived in Canada. He studied at McMaster University, Hamilton; Ohio State University; the University of Fribourg and the New School for Social

Research, New York. He is now Professor of Theology and Social Ethics at McGill University, Montreal. He is editor of *The Ecumenist*; his books include *Religion and Alienation* (1975), *The Social Imperative* (1978), *Catholics and Canadian Socialism* (1980), *The Priority of Labor* (1982), *Ethics and Economics* (1984) and *Theology and Society* (1987).
Address: McGill University, 3520 University St, Montreal H3A 2A7.

PAUL A. SOUKUP, SJ, an associate professor of communication at Santa Clara University (California), has studied and worked in church communication for over ten years. In addition to his teaching, he has served as a consultant to the Communication Committee of the United States Catholic Conference and to the Communication Office of the Diocese of Austin, Texas. He has published *Communication and Theology: An Introduction and Review of the Literature*, London 1983; *Christian Communication: A Bibliographical Survey*, New York 1989, and edited (with Bruce Gronbeck and Thomas J. Farrell), *Media, Consciousness and Culture*, Newbury Park, CA 1991, and (with Thomas J. Farrell), *Faith and Contexts [Essays of Walter J. Ong]*, Atlanta 1992.
Address: Communication Department, Santa Clara University, Santa Clara, CA 95053, USA.

OTTMAR FUCHS was born in 1945 and grew up in Erlangen; he studied philosophy and theology in Bamberg and Würzburg and was ordained priest in 1972. After nine years in pastoral work he gained his doctorate in pastoral theology in 1977 and his Habilitation in 1981, both in Würzburg. Since 1981 he has been Professor of Pastoral Theology and Kerygmatics in the University of Bamberg. Recent publications include: *Kirche Kabel Kapital. Standpunkte einer christlichen Medienpolitik*, Münster 1989; *Zwischen Wahrhaftigkeit und Macht. Pluralismus in der Kirche*, Frankfurt 1990; *God's People: Instruments of Healing. The Diaconical Dimension of the Church*, Bern 1993; *Ämter für eine Kirche der Zukunft*, Fribourg CH 1993.
Address: Universität Bamberg, Postfach 1549, D–8600 Bamberg, Germany.

MICHAEL A. RUSSO, Ph.D., is Chairman of the Communications Department at Saint Mary's College of California. In 1990, he was appointed a Joan Shorenstein Barone Fellow at the John F. Kennedy School of Government, Harvard University. He has worked for CBS News as a producer and consultant on political and religious news broadcasts. He is a

priest and serves the parish community of Saint Joseph the Worker, Berkeley, California.
Address: Saint Mary's College, Dept of Communication, Moraga, California 94575, USA.

KENNETH L. WOODWARD is a senior writer of *Newsweek* magazine, where he has also served as Religion Editor since 1964. He has also contributed articles, essays and reviews to *The New York Times*, *Commonweal*, *America* and other publications. He is the author of *Making Saints: How the Catholic Church Determines Who Becomes a Saint, Who Doesn't and Why*, New York 1990, and the co-author with Arthur Kornhaber of *Grandparents/Grandchildren: The Vital Connection*, New York 1981.
Address: *Newsweek*, 444 Madison Avenue, New York, NY 10022, USA.

ARND HENZE was born in 1961. He studied Protestant theology at the universities of Göttingen and Heidelberg and at the Graduate Theological Union in Berkeley, California; further studies have been concerned with sociological and international questions. He now works as a television editor for Westdeutscher Rundfunk. He has written numerous social reports and documentaries.
Address: Dellbrücker Mauspfad 2361, 5000 Köln 80, Deutschland.

Members of the Advisory Committee for Sociology of Religion

Directors

John Coleman SJ	Berkeley, CA	USA
Miklós Tomka	Budapest	Hungary

Members

Sabino Acquaviva	Padua	Italy
Gregory Baum	Montreal	Canada
Silvano Burgalassi	Pisa	Italy
Joan Chittister OSB	Erie, PA	USA
Gérard Defois	Paris	France
Karel Dobbelaere	Louvain	Belgium
Jacques Grand'Maison	Montreal	Canada
Andrew Greeley	Chicago, IL	USA
Barbara Hargrove	Denver, CO	USA
Franz-Xavier Kaufmann	Bielefeld	Germany
Leonardus Laeyendecker	Leiden	The Netherlands
David Martin	London	Great Britain
Peter McAffery	Old Aberdeen	Great Britain
Meredith McGuire	San Antonio, TX	USA
Ferdinand Menne	Münster	Germany
John Orme Mills OP	Oxford	Great Britain
Hans Mol	Hamilton, Ont.	Canada
Marie Neal SND	Boston, MA	USA
Jean Remy	Louvain-la-Neuve	Belgium
Rudolf Siebert	Kalamazoo, MI	USA
Jean-Guy Vaillancourt	Montreal	Canada
Conor Ward	Dublin	Ireland

Concilium

Issues of *Concilium* to be published in 1994

1994/1: Violence against Women

Edited by Elisabeth Schüssler Fiorenza and M. Shawn Copeland

This issue aims not only to raise church consciousness about the existence of widespread violence against women but also to explore its significance for a feminist rearticulation of Christian theology. Accounts of women's experiences of violence are followed by discussions of cultural identity values, including the pornographic exploitation of women; a third part discusses the church's encouragement of violence against women and the issue ends with new means of feminine empowerment.

03024 2   *February*

1994/2: Christianity and Culture: A Mutual Enrichment

Edited by Norbert Greinacher and Norbert Mette

This issue explores that point in the relationship between Christianity and cultures where a culture discloses new dimensions of the gospel as well as being the object of criticism in the light of the gospel, a process known as 'inculturation'. Part One examines fundamental aspects of inculturation, Part Two looks at test cases (in Coptic Christianity, Zaire, Pakistan, Latin America and Canada) and Part Three reflects thinking on inculturation.

03025 0   *April*

1994/3   Islam: A Challenge for Christianity

Edited by Hans Küng and Jürgen Moltmann

The first section describes experiences of Islam in Africa, Central Asia, Indonesia, Pakistan and Europe and the second the threat felt by Christians from Islam and by Muslims from Christianity. The final section explores the challenges posed by Islam; monotheism, the unity of religion and politics, Islamic views of human rights and the position Islam occupies as a religion coming into being after Christianity and Judaism.

03026 9   *June*

1994/4: Mysticism and the Institutional Crisis
Edited by Christian Duquoc and Gustavo Gutiérrez

The decline in mainstream church membership suggests that a less institutional and more mystical approach to religion is called for, and that this is an approach which the churches should encourage. This issue looks at mystical movements in various parts of the globe, from Latin America through Africa to Asia, and asks how they can become less marginalized than they have been in the past.

03022 7   August

1994/5: Catholic Identity
Edited by James Provost and Knut Walf

How is an institution, a movement, a social teaching, or even an individual 'Catholic' today? The question has many applications, in terms of identity, discipline, teaching and so on. This issue explores its ramifications with relation to particular theological and canonical issues.

03028 5   October

1994/6: Why Theology?
Edited by Werner Jeanrond and Claude Jeffré

This issue surveys the programme, methods and audience for theology today, at a time when its status as an academic discipline is no longer possible, and in many contexts it cannot be engaged in without interference from state and church authorities.

03029 3   December

Titles for Issues to be Published in 1995

Concilium Subscription Information - outside North America

Individual Annual Subscription (six issues): £30.00

Institution Annual Subscription (six issues): £40.00

Airmail subscriptions: add £10.00

Individual issues: £8.95 each

New subscribers please return this form:
for a two-year subscription, double the appropriate rate

(for individuals)   £30.00   (1/2 years)   . . . .

(for institutions)   £40.00   (1/2 years)   . . . .

Airmail postage
outside Europe +£10.00   (1/2 years)   . . . .

                              Total . . . .

I wish to subscribe for one/two years as an individual/institution
(delete as appropriate)

Name/Institution . . . .

Address . . . .

. . . .

. . . .

I enclose a cheque for .... payable to SCM Press Ltd

Please charge my Access/Visa/Mastercard no. . . . .

Signature . . . . .Expiry Date . . . .

Please return this form to:
SCM PRESS LTD 26-30 Tottenham Road, London N1 4BZ